Essential

ARABIC
Speak Arabic With Confidence

TUTTLE Publishing

Tokyo | Rutland, Vermont | Singapore

Published by Tuttle Publishing, an imprint of
Periplus Editions (HK) Ltd.

www.tuttlepublishing.com

ISBN: 978-0-8048-4239-6

Distributed by
North America, Latin America & Europe
Tuttle Publishing
364 Innovation Drive
North Clarendon, VT 05759-9436 U.S.A.
Tel: 1 (802) 773-8930; Fax: 1 (802) 773-6993
info@tuttlepublishing.com
www.tuttlepublishing.com

Japan
Tuttle Publishing
Yaekari Building, 3rd Floor, 5-4-12 Osaki
Shinagawa-ku, Tokyo 141 0032
Tel: (81) 3 5437-0171; Fax: (81) 3 5437-0755
sales@tuttle.co.jp;   www.tuttle.co.jp

Asia Pacific
Berkeley Books Pte. Ltd.
61 Tai Seng Avenue #02-12, Singapore 534167
Tel: (65) 6280-1330; Fax: (65) 6280-6290
inquiries@periplus.com.sg;   www.periplus.com

Indonesia
PT Java Books Indonesia
Jl. Rawa Gelam IV No. 9
Kawasan Industri Pulogadung, Jakarta 13930
Tel: (62) 21 4682-1088; Fax: (62) 21 461-0206
crm@periplus.co.id   www.periplus.com

First edition
17 16 15 14   10 9 8 7 6 5 4 3   1411HP
Printed in Singapore

TUTTLE PUBLISHING® is a registered trademark
of Tuttle Publishing, a division of Periplus Editions
(HK) Ltd.

The Tuttle Story
"Books to Span the East and West"

Many people are surprised to learn that the world's largest publisher of books on Asia had its humble beginnings in the tiny American state of Vermont. The company's founder, Charles E. Tuttle, belonged to a New England family steeped in publishing.

Immediately after WWII, Tuttle served in Tokyo under General Douglas MacArthur and was tasked with reviving the Japanese publishing industry. He later founded the Charles E. Tuttle Publishing Company, which thrives today as one of the world's leading independent publishers.

Though a westerner, Tuttle was hugely instrumental in bringing a knowledge of Japan and Asia to a world hungry for information about the East. By the time of his death in 1993, Tuttle had published over 6,000 books on Asian culture, history and art—a legacy honored by the Japanese emperor with the "Order of the Sacred Treasure," the highest tribute Japan can bestow upon a non-Japanese.

With a backlist of 1,500 titles, Tuttle Publishing is more active today than at any time in its past—inspired by Charles Tuttle's core mission to publish fine books to span the East and West and provide a greater understanding of each.

Contents

Introduction

● ●

● **Welcome to the Tuttle Essential Language series, covering all of the most popular world languages. These books are basic guides in communicating in the language. They're concise, accessible and easy to understand, and you'll find them indispensable on your trip abroad to get you where you want to go, pay the right prices and do everything you've been planning to do.**

This guide is divided into 17 themed sections and starts with a pronunciation table which explains the phonetic pronunciation to all the words and sentences you'll need to know, and a basic grammar guide which will help you construct basic sentences in Arabic. At the end of this book is an extensive English–Arabic word list.

Throughout the book you'll come across boxes with a ✋ beside them. These are designed to help you if you can't understand what your listener is saying to you. Hand the book over to them and encourage them to point to the appropriate answer to the question you are asking.

Other boxes in the book—this time without the symbol—give alphabetical listings of themed words with their English translations beside them.

For extra clarity, we have put all phonetic pronunciations of the foreign language terms in italic.

This book covers all subjects you are likely to come across during the course of a visit, from reserving a room for the night to ordering food and drink at a restaurant and what to do if your car breaks down or you lose your traveler's checks and money. With over 2,000 commonly used words and essential sentences at your fingertips you can rest assured that you will be able to get by in all situations, so let *Essential Arabic* become your passport to learning to speak with confidence!

Pronunciation guide

The imitated pronunciation should be read as if it were English, bearing in mind that the emphatic consonants indicate more a vowel volume than a separate sound.

English	Arabic	Phonetic Description	Approximate in English
b	ب	voiced labial stop	b as in bad
d	د	voiced alveolar stop	as in dad
d	ض	emphatic voiced alveolar stop	does not exist (similar to Don)
f	ف	voiceless labio-dental fricative	as in fat
h	هـ	voiceless glottal fricative	as in hat
h	ح	voiceless pharyngeal fricative	does not exist
j	ج	voiced palato-alveolar fricative	as in jelly
k	ك	voiceless velar stop	as in kick
l	ل	alveolar lateral	as in lick
m	م	bilabial nasal	as in might
n	ن	alveolar nasal	as in night
q	ق	uvular stop	does not exist
r	ر	alveolar trill	as in right
s	س	voiceless alveolar fricative	as in sight
s	ص	emphatic voiceless alveolar fricative	does not exist (similar to Sahara)
t	ت	voiceless dental fricative	as in tight
t	ط	emphatic voiceless alveolar stop	does not exist (similar to Tokyo)
z	ز	voiced alveolar fricative	as in zebra
z	ظ	emphatic voiced alveolar fricative	dh or z (depends on region)
'	أ, ء	glottal stop	a

English	Arabic	Phonetic Description	Approximate in English
'	ع	voiced pharyngeal fricative	does not exist
sh	ش	voiceless palato-alveolar fricative	as in *shoes*
th	ث	voiceless dental fricative	as in *three*
dh	ذ	voiced dental fricative	as in *there*
kh	خ	voiceless velar fricative	does not exist
gh	غ	voiced velar fricative	does not exist
y	ي	palatal glide	as in *yellow*
w	و	bilabial approximant	as in *wall*

Vowels: there are three basic short vowels in Arabic and three long ones. These are:

Vowel	Phonetic description	English equivalent
a	short low back vowel	as in *Amsterdam*
aa	long low back vowel	as in *far*
i	short high front vowel	as in *inside*
ii	long high front vowel	as in *clean*
u	short high back vowel	as in *to go*
uu	long high back vowel	as in *noon*

Stressing of words

Arabic words do not have a stressed syllable in the manner that English words do. However, individual consonants can exhibit stress by means of a **shadda** (gemination)—this is represented by a duplicated consonant. For example, in the word **kassara** "to break," the duplicated **s** indicates consonantal stress as in the English name **Cassandra**.

Basic grammar

There are two genders in Arabic, masculine (m.) and feminine (f.). This applies to verbs, nouns and adjectives.

Verbs

There are two different types of verb in Arabic, depending on their tense/mood: perfective (action complete) and imperfective (action incomplete). Verbs are marked for person, number and gender.

In Arabic first, second and third persons are marked differently in the verb form, e.g. *anna adresu* 'I study,' *anta tadresu* 'you study,' *huwas yadresu* 'he studies.'

Verbs inherently exhibit gender marking in both perfective (past) and imperfective (present) forms. In the perfective form masculine gender is unmarked, whereas feminine gender is shown by a final *t* sound, e.g. *'al-waladu 'akala* 'the boy ate' compared with *'al-bintu 'akalat* 'the girl ate'. In the imperfective form gender is shown by means of prefixes using the *t* and *y* sounds to indicate respectively masculine and feminine genders, e.g. *'al-waladu ya'kulu* 'the boy eats/is eating' compared with *'al-bintu ta'kulu* 'the girl eats/is eating.'

Nouns

There are two types of noun in Arabic. One is known as regular, where the feminine form can be derived from the masculine form, for example:

	Masculine	Feminine
'Student'	*taalib*	*taalibat*
'Teacher'	*mudarris*	*mudarrisat*
'Driver'	*saa'iq*	*saa'iqat*

The other class of nouns is irregular, where the masculine and feminine forms do not share the same root and cannot be derived from one another. These should be learned gradually as individual items of vocabulary. Examples of this type of noun are *walad* 'boy,' *bint* 'girl'; *imra'at* 'woman', *rajul* 'man.'

Note that even non-human nouns are obligatorily marked for gender, e.g. *daar* (f.) 'house,' *madiinat* (f.) 'city,' *balad* (m.) 'country,' *qalam* (m.) 'pen.'

Arabic differentiates between singular, dual and plural numbers, although the dual form is not used frequently. The dual and the regular plural can be derived from the singular form as shown below:

	Root	Singular	Dual	Plural
'Player'	*l-'-b*	*laa'ib*	*laa'ib**aan***	*laa'ib**uun***
'Teacher'	*d-r-s*	*mudarris*	*mudarris**aan***	*mudarris**uun***
'Spectator'	*f-r-j*	*mutafarrij*	*mutafarrij**aan***	*mutafarrij**uun***

The above examples relate to the masculine gender only. Feminine derived nouns take the suffix *–at* in the singular form and replace the masculine plural suffix *–uun* with the feminine plural suffix *–aat*; for example *mudarrisat* 'female teacher' becomes *mudarrisaat* 'female teachers.' The feminine dual form is similar to the masculine form withthe exception of the feminine marker *–at* being inserted before the dual suffix, e.g. *mudarrisataan* 'two female teachers.'

Definiteness in Arabic is marked in general by means of the article *al-* attached at the beginning of the noun, e.g. *walad* 'a boy,' *al-walad* 'the boy.' However, with a number of consonants, known as the solar consonants, a sound harmony rule means that the final sound of the article is assimilated to the first consonant of the noun, e.g. *sayyaarat* 'a car,' *as-sayyaarat* 'the car.' The consonants to which this applies are *d, dh, d, t, t, th, s, sh, s, z, z, n, l* and *r*.

'Case' refers to the grammatical function assigned to the noun. In Arabic there are three essential case markings—nominative (when the noun is the subject of the sentence), accusative (when the noun is the object of the sentence) and genitive (when the noun is the object of a preposition). Case marking is shown differently depending on the definite or indefinite status of the noun, as shown below for the noun *walad* 'boy':

	Nominative	Accusative	Genitive
Definite	*al-waladu*	*al-walada*	*al-waladi*
Indefinite	*waladun*	*waladan*	*waladin*

Adjectives

Adjectives tend to go after the noun to which they refer. They must agree with the noun they accompany in gender (masculine or feminine), number (singular, dual or plural) and case (nominative, accusative or genitive), e.g. *al-waladu an-najiibu najaha* 'the studious boy passed (the exam)'; *qaabaltu al-walada an-najiiba* 'I met the studious boy.'

Possessive adjectives

Possessive adjectives agree in gender and number with the noun to which they relate (the owner), as in English. They cannot be used in conjunction with the definite article. The following examples using the word *kitaab* 'book' illustrate the way possessives are marked in Arabic.

kitaab-ii	'my book'
kitaabu-ka	'your (m. sing.) book'
kitaabu-ki	'your (f. sing.) book'
kitaabu-hu	'his book'
kitaabu-ha	'her book'
kitaabu-kumaa	'your (dual) book'
kitaabu-humaa	'their (dual) book'
kitaabu-naa	'our book'
kitaabu-kum	'your (m. pl.) book'
kitaabu-kunna	'your (f. pl.) book'
kitaabu-hum	'their (m. pl.) book'
kitaabu-hunna	'their (f. pl.) book'

Personal pronouns

Since verb endings (*-tu*, *-ta*, *-ti*, *-tum*, etc) can be sufficient to indicate who is doing the action, personal pronouns are not always used. However, to avoid confusion, you should use them. The Arabic personal pronouns are:

I	*anaa*
you (m. sing.)	*anta*
you (f. sing.)	*anti*
he	*huwa*
she	*huya*
you (dual)	*antumaa*
they (dual)	*umaa*
we	*nahnu*
you (m. pl.)	*antum*
you (f. pl.)	*antunna*
they (m.)	*hum*
they (f.)	*hunna*

Forming questions

The easiest way of asking a question in Arabic is by using one of a number of question words at the beginning of the statement or phrase. However, the type of question word used depends on the sentence or phrase itself (similar to English in its distinction between 'do/does' and 'what/why,' etc). The following are examples of the most frequent question words: **maa haadha** 'what's this?'; **ayyat imra'a** 'which lady?'; **ay rajul** 'which man?'; **man anta** 'who are you?'

Examples of turning a declarative sentence (statement) into an interrogative one (question):

akala al-waladu 'the boy ate'
    —> **hal** *akala al-waladu* 'did the boy eat?'

kharajat al-bintu 'the girl left'
    —> **limaadhaa** *kharajat al-bintu* 'why did the girl leave?'

habatat at-taa'ira 'the plane landed'
    —> **mataa** *habatat at-taa'ira* 'when did the plane land?'

ishtaraa qamiis 'he bought a shirt'
    —> **ayna** *ishtaraa qamiis* 'where did he buy a shirt?'

Forming negative sentences

As with forming questions, negation is expressed differently for nominal as opposed to verbal sentences.

When negating nominal and adjectival phrases, *laysa* and its variants are used as shown below. The nominal negation word *laysa* is always inserted after the pronoun or noun to which it refers, e.g. **lastu ghaadiban** 'not I angry,' i.e. 'I am not angry.'

Here are the various forms of *laysa* with the main pronouns:

anaa	I	*lastu*
anta	you (m. sing.)	*lasta*
anti	you (f. sing.)	*lasti*
huwa	he	*laysa*
hiya	she	*laysat*
nahnu	we	*lasnaa*
antum	you (m. pl.)	*astum*
antunna	you (f. pl.)	*lastunna*
hum	they (m.)	*laysuu*

There are four verbal negation words used to negate verbal actions in the present, past and the future respectively. These are shown in the following examples:

laa	present	**laa ashrab**	I don't write.
lan	future	**lan shrab**	I won't drink.
lam	past	**lam ashrab**	I did not drink.
maa	past/continuing	**maa sharibtu**	I have not drunk.

1 The Basics

1. The Basics

1.1 Personal details

surname	*al-laqab/ism al-'aa'ila* اللقب/اسم العائلة
first name	*al-ism* الاسم
initials	*mukhtasar al-ism* مختصر الاسم
address (street/number)	*al-'unwaan/ism wa raqam ash-shaari'* العنوان (اسم ورقم الشارع)
postal (zip) code/town	*ar-raqm al-bariidi/al-madiina* المدينة/الرقم البريدي
phone number	*raqam al-haatif* رقم الهاتف
sex (male/female)	*al-jins (dhakar/unthaa)* الجنس (ذكر/أنثى)
nationality	*al-jinsiyya* الجنسية
date of birth	*taariikh al-wilaada* تاريخ الولادة
place of birth	*makaan al-wilaada* مكان الولادة
occupation	*al-mihna* المهنة
marital status	*al-haala al-madaniyya* الحالة المدنية
married/single	*mutazawwij/a'zab* متزوج/أعزب

widowed	*armala*
	أرملة
(number of) children	*'adad al-atfaal*
	عدد الأطفال
passport/identity card/ driving license number	*jawaaz safar/bitaaqa shakhsiyya/* *raqam rukhsat as-siyaaqa*
	جواز سفر/بطاقة شخصية/ رقم رخصة السياقة
place and date of issue	*mahal wa taariikh as-suduur*
	محل وتاريخ الصدور
signature	*at-tawqii'*
	التوقيع

1.2 Today or tomorrow?

What day is it today?	*Maa l-yawm?*
	ما اليوم؟
Today's Monday	*Al-yawm al-'ithnayn*
	اليوم الاثنين
– Tuesday	*ath-thulaathaa'*
	الثلاثاء
– Wednesday	*al-'arbi'aa'*
	الأربعاء
– Thursday	*al-khamiis*
	الخميس
– Friday	*al-jumu'a*
	الجمعة
– Saturday	*as-sabt*
	السبت
– Sunday	*al-'ahad*
	الأحد

in January	*fii kaanuun ath-thaanii* في كانون الثاني
since February	*mundhu shahr shubaat* منذ شهر شباط
in spring	*fii ar-rabii'* في الربيع
in summer	*fii as-sayf* في الصيف
in autumn	*fii al-khariif* في الخريف
in winter	*fii ash-shitaa'* في الشتاء
2012	*Alfaan wa ithnata 'asharata* ألفان واثنتا عشرة
2013	*Alfaan wa thalaathata 'ashara* ألفان وثلاثة عشر
2014	*Alfaan wa arba'ata 'ashara* ألفان وأربعة عشر
the twentieth century	*al-qarnu al-'ishruun* القرن العشرون
the twenty-first century	*al-qarnu al-haadii wa al-'ishruun* القرن الحادي والعشرون
What's the date today?	*Maa huwa taariikhu al-yawm?* ما هو التاريخ اليوم؟
Today's the twenty-fourth	*Al-yawm huwa ar-raabi' wa al-'ishruun* اليوم هو الرابع والعشرون
Monday 3 November	*Al-ithnayn thalaatha tishriin ath-thaanii* الاثنين ثلاث تشرين الثاني
in the morning	*fii as-sabaah* في الصباح

in the afternoon	*ba'da az-zuhr* بعد الظهر
in the evening	*fii al-masaa'* في المساء
at night	*fii al-layl* في الليل
this morning	*haadhaa as-sabaah* هذا الصباح
this afternoon	*ba'da zuhr al-yawm* بعد ظهر اليوم
this evening	*haadhaa al-masaa'* هذا المساء
tonight	*haadhihi al-layla* هذه الليلة
last night	*al-baariha* البارحة
this week	*haadhaa al-usbuu'* هذا الأسبوع
next month	*ash-shahr al-qaadim* الشهر القادم
last year	*as-sana al-maadiya* السنة الماضية
next...	*al-qaadim* القادم
in...days/weeks/months/ years	*khilaal...ai-yam/asaabii'/shuhoor/ siniin* خلال...أيام/أسابيع/شهور/سنين
weeks ago	*mundhu asaabii'* منذ أسابيع

| day off | yawm ijaaza |
| | يوم إجازة |

1.3 What time is it?

What time is it?	Kam as-saa'a al'aan?
	كم الساعة الان؟
It's nine o'clock	As-saa'a at-taasi'a
	الساعة التاسعة
– five past ten	al-'aashira wa khams daqaa'iq
	العاشرة وخمس دقائق
– a quarter past eleven	al-haadiya 'ashra wa ar-rub'
	الحادية عشرة والربع
– twenty past twelve	ath-thaaniya 'ashara wa ath-thulth ('ishruun daqiiqa)
	الثانية عشرة والثلث (وعشرون دقيقة)
– half past one	al-waahida wa an-nisf
	الواحدة والنصف
– twenty-five to three	ath-thaaniya wa khamsa wa thalaathuun daqiiqa
	الثانية وخمسة وثلاثون دقيقة
– a quarter to four	ar-raabi'a illaa rubu'an
	الرابعة الاربعا
– ten to five	al-khaamisa illaa 'ashr daqaa'iq
	الخامسة إلا عشر دقائق
It's midday (twelve noon)	Muntasafu an-nahaar
	منتصف النهار
It's midnight	Muntasafu al-layl
	منتصف الليل

half an hour	*nisf saa'a* نصف ساعة
What time?	*Mataa?* متى؟
What time can I come by?	*Mataa astatii' an a'tii?* متى أستطيع أن آتي؟
At...	*'inda...* عند...
After...	*ba'da...* بعد...
Before...	*qabla...* قبل...
Between...and...	*bayna as-saa'a...wa...* بين الساعة...و...
From...to...	*min...ilaa...* من...إلى...
In...minutes	*khilaal...daqaa'iq* خلال...دقائق
– an hour	*saa'a waahida* ساعة واحدة
– ...hours	*...saa'aat* ساعات...
– a quarter of an hour	*rub'u saa'a* ربع ساعة
– three quarters of an hour	*thalaathat arbaa' as-saa'a* ثلاثة أرباع الساعة
too early/late	*muta'akhir/mubakkiran kathiiran* متأخر/مبكرا كثيرا
on time	*fii alwaw'id tamaaman* في الموعد تماما

summertime (daylight saving)	*at-tawqiit as-sayfii* التوقيت الصيفي
wintertime	*at-tawqiit ash-shitwii* التوقيت الشتوي

1.4 One, two, three...

0	*sifr* صفر
1	*waahid* واحد
2	*ithnaan* اثنان
3	*thalaatha* ثلاثة
4	*arba'a* أربعة
5	*khamsa* خمسة
6	*sitta* ستة
7	*sab'a* سبعة
8	*thamaaniya* ثمانية
9	*tis'a* تسعة
10	*'ashara* عشرة
11	*ahada 'ashar* أحد عشر
12	*ithnay 'ashara* اثنى عشر
13	*thalaathata 'ashara* ثلاثة عشر
14	*arba'ata 'ashara* أربعة عشر
15	*khamsat 'ashara* خمسة عشر
16	*sittaat 'ashara* ستة عشر
17	*sab'ata 'ashara* سبعة عشر
18	*thamaaniyata 'ashara* ثمانية عشر
19	*tis'ata 'ashara* تسعة عشر
20	*'ishruun* عشرون
21	*waahid wa 'ishruun* واحد وعشرون

22	*ithnaan wa 'ishruun*	اثنان وعشرون
30	*thalaathuun*	ثلاثون
31	*waahid wa thalaathuun*	واحد وثلاثون
32	*ithnaan wa thalaathuun*	اثنان وثلاثون
40	*arba'uun*	أربعون
50	*khamsuun*	خمسون
60	*sittuun*	ستون
70	*sab'uun*	سبعون
80	*thamaanuun*	ثمانون
90	*tis'uun*	تسعون
100	*mi'a*	مئة
101	*mi'a wa waahid*	مئة وواحد
110	*mi'a wa 'ashara*	مئة وعشرة
120	*mi'a wa 'ishruun*	مئة وعشرون
200	*mi'ataan*	مئتان
300	*thalaathumi'a*	ثلاثمئة
400	*arba'umi'a*	أربعمئة
500	*khamsumi'a*	خمسمئة
600	*sittumi'a*	ستمئة
700	*sab'umi'a*	سبعمئة
800	*thamaanimi'a*	ثمانمئة
900	*tis'umi'a*	تسعمئة
1000	*'alf*	ألف
1100	*'alf wa mi'a*	ألف ومئة
2000	*'alfaan*	ألفان
10,000	*'ashrat 'alaaf*	عشرة آلاف
100,000	*mi'at 'alf*	مئة ألف
1,000,000	*malyuun*	مليون

1st	al-awwal	الأول
2nd	ath-thaanii	الثاني
3rd	ath-thaalith	الثالث
4th	ar-raabi'	الرابع
5th	al-khaamis	الخامس
6th	as-saadis	السادس
7th	as-saabi'	السابع
8th	ath-thaamin	الثامن
9th	at-taasi'	التاسع
10th	al-'aashir	العاشر
11th	al-haadii 'ashar	الحادي عشر
12th	ath-thaanii 'ashar	الثاني عشر
13th	ath-thaalith 'ashar	الثالث عشر
14th	ar-rabi' 'ashar	الرابع عشر
15th	al-khaamis 'ashar	الخامس عشر
16th	as-saadis 'ashar	السادس عشر
17th	as-saabi' 'ashar	السابع عشر
18th	ath-thamin 'ashar	الثامن عشر
19th	at-taasi' 'ashar	التاسع عشر
20th	al-'ishruun	العشرون
21st	al-haadii wa al-'ishruun	الحادي والعشرون
22nd	ath-thaanii wa al-'ishruun	الثاني والعشرون
30th	ath-thalaathuun	الثلاثون
100th	al-mi'a	المئة
1,000th	al-'alf	الألف
once	marra waahida	مرة واحدة
twice	marratayn	مرتين
double	di'f	ضعف

triple	*thalaathat ad'aaf* ثلاثة أضعاف
half	*nisf* نصف
a quarter	*rub'* ربع
a third	*thuluth* ثلث
some/a few	*ba'd/bid'u* بعض/بضع
2 + 4 = 6	*Ithnayn zaa'id arba'a yusaawii sitta* اثنين زائد أربعة يساوي ستة
4 – 2 = 2	*Arba'a naaqis ithnayn yusaawii ithnayni* أربعة ناقص اثنين يساوي اثنين
2 x 4 = 8	*Arba'a daarib ithnayn yusaawii thamaaniya* اثنان في أربعة يساوي ثمانية
4 ÷ 2 = 2	*Arba'a 'alaa ithnayn yusaawii ithnayn* أربعة على اثنين يساوي اثنين
even/odd	*Fardiy/zawjiy* فردي/زوجي
total	*Majmuu'* مجموع
6 x 9	*Tis'a daarib sitta* ستة في تسعة

1.5 The weather

Is the weather going to be good/bad?	*Hal sayakuun at-taqs jayyid/sayyi'?* هل سيكون الطقس جيداً/سيئاً؟
Is it going to get colder/hotter?	*Hal sayakuun at-taqs abrad/ahar?* هل سيكون الطقس أبرد/احر؟
What temperature is it going to be?	*Kayfa satakuun darajatu l-haraara?* كيف ستكون درجة الحرارة؟
Is it going to rain?	*Hal satumtir?* هل ستمطر؟
Is there going to be a storm?	*Hal satakuun hunaaka 'aasifa?* هل ستكون هناك عاصفة؟

Is it going to snow?	*Hal sayatasaaqat ath-thalj?*
	هل سيتساقط الثلج؟
Is it going to freeze?	*Hal sayakuunu hunaaka tajallud?*
	هل سيكون هناك تجلد؟
Is the thaw setting in?	*Hal satadhuub ath-thuluuj?*
	هل ستذوب الثلوج؟
Is it going to be foggy?	*Hal sayakuunu hunaaka dabaab?*
	هل سيكون هناك ضباب؟
Is there going to be a thunderstorm?	*Hal satakuun hunaaka 'awaasif ra'diyya?*
	هل ستكون هناك عواصف رعدية؟
The weather's changing	*At-taqs mutaghayyir (mutaqallib)*
	الطقس متغير/متقلب
It's going to be cold	*Sayakuunu at-taqs baaridan*
	سيكون الطقس باردا
What's the weather going to be like today/ tomorrow?	*Kayfa sayakuunu at-taqs al-yawm/ ghadan?*
	كيف سيكون الطقس اليوم/غدا؟

حر شديد جدا/رطب	بارد	مطر
har shadiid jiddan/ratib	*baarid*	*matar*
sweltering/muggy	cool	rain
مشمس	صقيع	صافي/صحو
mushmis	*saqii'*	*saafi/sahw*
sunny	frost	fine/clear
جيد/حسن	صقيع في الليل	خانق
jayyid/hasan	*saqii' fii l-layl*	*khaaniq*
fine	overnight frost	stifling
تجمد/متجمد	جليد/ثلجي	عاصفة
tajammud/mutajammid	*jaliid/thalj*	*'aasifa*
frost/frosty	ice/icy	storm

حار جدا **haar jiddan** very hot	بارد ورطب **baarid wa ratib** cold and damp	رطب **ratib** humid
مطر غزير **matar ghaziir** heavy rain	برد **barad** hail	إعصار **i'saar** hurricane
...درجات فوق/تحت الصفر **...darajaat fawqa/tahta as-sifr** ...degrees below/above zero	لطيف **latiif** mild	رياح **riyaah** wind
سماء صافية/غائمة **samaa' saafiya/ghaa'ima** clear skies/cloudy	ثلج **thalj** snow	موجة حر **mawjat har** heatwave
انهمار المطر **inhimaar al-matar** downpour	غائم **ghaa'im** cloudiness	عاصف **'aasif** windy
يوم مشمس **yawmun mushmis** sunny day	مكشوف **makshuuf** bleak	غيوم **ghuyuum** clouds
رياح متوسطة السرعة/ قوية/قوية جدا **riyaah mutawassitat as-sur'a/** **qawiyya/qawiyya jidan** moderate/strong/ very strong winds	عصفة ريح **'asfat riih** gusts of wind	برق **Barq** Lightning
	ضباب/ضبابي **dabaab/dabaabi** fog/foggy	رعد **ra'd** thunder

Here, there...

See also 5.1 Asking directions

Where is the book?   **Ayna al-kitaab?**
أين الكتاب؟

beside/next to	*bijaanib* بجانب
between . . . and . . .	*baina . . . wa . . .* بين . . . . و . . . .
middle/center	*wasat* وسط
Kansas in the middle/ center of America	*Kansas fii wasat amreeka* كانساس في وسط أمريكا
here/there	*hunaa/hunaak* هنا/هناك
somewhere/nowhere	*fii makaanin maa/ghayr mawjuud* في مكان ما/غير موجود
everywhere	*fii kul makaan* في كل مكان
far away/nearby	*ba'iid/qariib* بعيد/قريب
(on the) right/(on the) left	*'alaa al-yamiin/al-yasaar* على اليمين/اليسار
to the right/left of...	*ilaa yamiin/yasaar al-...* الى يمين/يسار ال...
straight ahead	*mubaasharatan* مباشرة
via	*'an tariiq* عن طريق
in/to	*fii/ilaa* في/إلى
on	*'alaa* على
under	*tahta* تحت

against	*'aks*
	عكس
opposite/facing	*muqaabil/muwaajih*
	مقابل/مواجه
next to	*bil-qurbi min*
	بالقرب من
near	*qurba*
	قرب
in front of	*amaama*
	أمام
in the center	*fii al-markaz*
	في المركز
forward	*ilaa al-amaam*
	إلى الأمام
down	*asfal*
	أسفل
up	*a'laa/fawq*
	فوق/أعلى
inside	*daakhil*
	داخل
outside	*khaarij*
	خارج
behind	*khalf*
	خلف
at the front	*fii al-muqaddima*
	في المقدمة
at the back/in line	*ilaa al-waraa'/fii as-saffi*
	الى الوراء/في الصف
in the north	*fii ash-shamaal*
	في الشمال

to the south	*ilaa al-januub* الى الجنوب
from the west	*min al-gharb* من الغرب
from the east	*min ash-sharq* من الشرق
to the...of	*ilaa al-...min* الى ال...من

1.7 What does that sign say?

See 5.4 Traffic signs

للإيجار *lil'iijaar* for hire	نافذ *naafidh* sold out	غرفة الحمام *ghurfat al-hammam* bathroom
ماء حار /بارد *maa' haar/baarid* hot/cold water	توقف اضطراري *tawaqquf idtiraari* emergency brake	غرفة انتظار *ghurfat intizaar* waiting room
ماء صالح/غير صالح الشرب *maa' saalih/ghayr saalih lish-shurb* no drinking water	الرجاء عدم الإزعاج اللمس *ar-rajaa' 'adam l-iz'aaj l-lamas* please do not disturb	مهرب من الحريق/ سلم ميكانيكي *mahrab min al-hariiq/sullam miikaaniikii* fire escape/escalator
للإيجار *lil'iijaar* for rent	عاطل *'aatil* out of order	ادفع *idfa'* push
قوة كهربائية عالية *quwwa kahrabaa- 'iyya 'aaliya* high voltage	للبيع *lil-bay'* for sale	اسحب *ishab* pull

فندق
funduq
hotel

قف
qif
stop

مفتوح
maftuuh
open

احذر الكلاب
ihdhar al-kilaab
beware of the dog

خطر
khatar
danger

محاسب/امين الصندوق
muhaasib/amiin as-sunduuq
cashier

مكتب تذاكر سفر
maktab tadhaakir safar
ticket office

شرطة
shurta
police

تصريف
tasriif
exchange

مملوء
mamluu'
full

غير قابل للاستعمال
ghayr qaabil lil'isti'maa
not in use

معلومات
ma'luumaat
information

اجرة الدخول
ujrat ad-dukhuul
entrance (free)

مشغول
mashghuul
engaged

جدول مواعيد
jadwal mawaa'iid
timetable

مستشفى
mustashfaa
hospital

شرطة المرور
shurtat al-muruur
traffic police

شرطة/البلدية
shurta/ al-baladiyya
(municipal) police

قسم الاطفاء
qism al-itfaa'
fire department

مشاة
mushaat
pedestrians

مكتب معلومات السياح
maktab ma'luumaat as-suyaah
tourist information bureau

مكتب البريد
maktab bariid
post office

مخرج طوارئ
makhraj tawaari'
(emergency) exit

محجوز
mahjuuz
reserved

مدخل
madkhal
entrance

إسعافات أولية/ حادث وطوارئ
is'aafat awwaliyya/ haadith wa tawaari'
first aid/accident and emergency (hospital)

ممنوع التدخين/لا ترم المهملات
mamnuu' at-tadkhiin/laa tarmi al-muhmalaat
no smoking/no litter

مغلق	ممنوع الدخول	خطر /خطر حريق/
mughlaq	**mamnuu'**	خطر على حياتك
closed (for holiday/ refurbishment)	**ad-dukhuul** no entry	**khatar/khatar hariiq/khatar 'alaa hayaatik**
ممنوع الصيد	دهن طري	danger/fire hazard/
mamnuu' as-sayd	**duhn tarii**	danger to life
no hunting/fishing	wet paint	

1.8 Legal holidays

Please note that for Islamic religious holidays, the dates change
from one year to another because the Muslim/lunar calendar is
ten days shorter than the Christian calendar (used throughout
the world). The dates listed for the Islamic holidays are for the
year 2013. The most important legal holidays in the Middle East
are the following:

January 1   New Year's Day
al-awwal min kaanuun ath-thaanii yawm ra's as-sana
١ كانون الثاني يوم رأس السنة

March/April   Easter and Easter Monday
nisaan/aadhar 'iid al-fis-h wa ithnayn al-fis-h
نيسان/آذار عيد الفصح و اثنين الفصح

1 May   Labor Day
al-awwal min ayaar 'iid al-'ummaal
١ أيار عيد العمال

9 July   Beginning of Ramadan
(Islamic holy month of fasting)
at-taasi' min tamuuz 'awwal, ramadaan
٩ تموز أول رمضان

8 August   Eid al-Fitr (End of Ramadan)
ath-thaamin min aab 'iidu l-fitr
٨ آب عيد الفطر

October 15	Eid Ul-idh-ha (Festival of Sacrifice)

October 15   Eid Ul-idh-ha (Festival of Sacrifice)
al-khaamis 'ashar min tishriin/'idul id-ha
١١ من تشرين/عيد الإضحى

November 4   Islamic New Year (Hijra)
ar-raabi' min tishriin ath-thaanii, ra's s-sana al-hijriyya
٤ تشرين الثاني رأس السنة الهجرية

25 December   Christmas Day
khamsa wa 'ishriin kaanuun al-awwal 'iidu l-miilaad
١٥ كانون الاول عيد الميلاد

Most shops, banks and government institutions are closed on
these days. Individual towns also have public holidays to celebrate their own patron saints.

1.9   Telephone alphabets

Pronouncing the alphabets:

b	*ba* ب	q	*qaaf* ق	th	*thaa'* ث
d	*dal* د	r	*raa'* ر	dh	*dhaal* ذ
d	*dad* ض	s	*siin* س	kh	*khaa'* خ
f	*faa'* ف	s	*saad* ص	gh	*ghayn* غ
h	*haa'* هـ	t	*taa'* ت	y	*yaa'* ي
h	*haa'* ح	t	*taa'* ط	w	*waaw* و
j	*jiim* ج	z	*zayn* ز		
k	*kaaf* ك	z	*zaa'* ظ		Vowels
l	*laam* ل	'	*hamza* ء	a	*fatha* ا
m	*miim* م	'	*ayn* ع	i	*kasra* ي
n	*nuun* ن	sh	*shiin* ش	u	*damma* و

2 Meet and Greet

2. Meet and Greet

● It is common in the Arab countries for men to shake hands on meeting and parting company. However, for religious and cultural reasons some women might not feel comfortable shaking hands with male strangers. Female friends and relatives may kiss each other on both cheeks when meeting and parting company. For men, this is also quite usual. When addressing men and women the terms **sayyid** and **sayyida** (meaning "Mr" and "Ms") are often used in more formal situations while **akh** and **ukht** (meaning "brother" and "sister") are used in more casual informal contexts.

2.1 Greetings

Hello/Good morning, Mr Williams	*Ahlan/sabaahu al-khayr sayyid wilyamz* أهلا/صباح الخير سيد وليام
Hello/Good morning, Mrs Jones	*Ahlan/sabaahu al-khayr sayyida jonz* أهلا/صباح الخير سيدة حونز
Hello, Peter	*Ahlan biitar* أهلا بيتر
Hi, Helen	*Ahlan hiiliin* أهلا هيلين
Welcome (to greet someone)	*Marhaban bika* مرحبا بك
Go ahead (please, be my guest)	*Tafaddal* تفضل
Good afternoon/evening	*Ahlan/masaa'u al-khayr* أهلا/مساء الخير
Hello/Good morning	*Ahlan/sabaahu al-khayr* أهلا/صباح الخير

How are you?/How are things?	*Kayfa haaluk?/kayfa umuuruk?* كيف حالك؟/كيف أمورك؟
Fine, thank you, and you?	*Bikhayr, shukran, wa anta?* بخير، شكرا، وأنت؟
Very well, and you?	*Jayyid jiddan, wa anta?* جيد جدا، وانت
In excellent health/ In great shape	*Fii sihha mumtaaza/fii haala mumtaaza* في صحة ممتازة/في حالة ممتازة
So-so	*Laa ba's* لابأس
Not very well	*Lastu 'alaa maa yuraam* لست على ما يرام
Not bad	*Laa ba'sa* لا بأس
I'm going to leave	*Anaa 'alaa washak an ughaadir* أنا على وشك أن أغادر
I have to be going, someone's waiting for me	*Yajib an adhhaba al'aan shakhsun maa yantazirunii* يجب أن أذهب الآن، شخص ما ينتظرني
Goodbye	*Ma'a s-salaama* مع السلامة
See you later	*Araaka fiimaa ba'd* أراك فيما بعد
See you soon	*Araaka qariiban* أراك قريبا
See you in a little while	*Araaka ba'da hiin* أراك بعد حين
Sweet dreams	*Ahlaam sa'iida* أحلام سعيدة

Good night	*Tusbih 'ala khayr*
	تصبح على خير
All the best	*Atamanna laka kulla khayr*
	أتمنى لك كل خير
Have fun	*Arjuu an tatasallaa jayyidan*
	أرجو أن تتسلى جيدا
Good luck	*Hazzan sa'iidan*
	حظا سعيدا
Have a nice vacation	*Atamanaa laka ijaaza sa'iida*
	أتمنى لك أجازة سعيدة
Have a good trip	*Atamanna laka rihla mumti'a*
	أتمنى لك رحلة مُتعة
Thank you, the same to you	*Shukran, wa anta kadhalika*
	شكرا، وأنت كذلك
Give my regards to... (formal)	*Balligh tahiyyaatii lii...*
	بلغ تحياتي ل...
Say hello to...(informal)	*Sallim 'alaa...*
	سلم على...

2.2 Asking a question

Who?	*Man?*
	من؟
Who's that?/Who is it?/ Who's there?	*Man dhaalik?/man huwa?/man hunaak?*
	من ذلك؟/من هو؟/من هناك؟
What?	*Maadhaa?*
	ماذا؟
What is this (f/m)?	*Maa haadhaa/haadhihi?*
	ما هذا/هذه؟

Is this your bag?	*Hal haadhihi haqiibatuka* هل هذه حقيبتك؟
What is there to see?	*Maadhaa hunaaka linaraa?* ماذا هناك لنرى؟
What category of hotel is it?	*Maa naw' (darajat)haadhaa al-funduq?* مانوع (درجة) هذا الفندق؟
Where?	*Ayna?* أين؟
Where's the bathroom?	*Ayna ghurfatu al-hammaam?* أين غرفة الحمام؟
Where are you going?	*Ilaa ayna anta dhaahib?* إلى أين انت ذاهب؟
Where are you from?	*Min ayyi balad anta?* من أي بلد انت؟
Where can I find a barber?	*Ayna yumkin an ajida hallaqan?* أين يمكن أن أجد حلاقا؟
What?/How?	*Maadhaa/kayfa?* ماذا؟/كيف؟
How far is that?	*Kam ya'bud dhaalik?* كم يبعد ذلك؟
How long does that take?	*Kam sa-yastaghriq dhaalik?* كم سيستغرق ذلك؟
How long is the trip?	*Kam sa-tastaghriq ar-rihla?* كم ستستغرق الرحلة؟
How much is this?	*Kam si'ru haadhaa?* كم سعر هذا؟
What time is it?	*Kam al-waqtu al-aan?* كم الوقت الأن؟
Which one(s)?	*Ay waahid/ay...?* أي واحد/أي؟

Which glass is mine?	*Ay ka'sin lii?* أي كأس لي؟
When?	*Mataa?* متى؟
When are you leaving?	*Mataa sa-tughaadir?* متى ستغادر؟
Why?	*Limaadhaa?* لماذا؟
Could you...?	*Hal yumkin...min fadlik?* هل يمكن...من فضلك؟
Could you help me, please?	*Hal yumkin an tusaa'idani min fadlik?* هل يمكن أن تساعدني من فضلك؟
Could you point that out to me/show me, please?	*Hal yumkin an tubayyina lii dhaalika/ turiyanii dhaalik min fadlik?* هل يمكن أن تبين لى ذلك/تريني ذلك من فضلك؟
Could you come with me, please?	*Hal yumkin an ta'tiya ma'ii min fadlik?* هل يمكن أن تأتي معي من فضلك؟
Could you book me some tickets, please?	*Hal yumkin tahjiza lii tadhaakira safar min fadlik?* هل يمكن أن تحجز لي تذاكر سفر من فضلك؟
Could you recommend another hotel?	*Hal tansahunii bi-funduq aakhar?* هل تنصحني بفندق آخر؟
Do you know...?	*Min fadlik, hal ta'rif...?* من فضلك، هل تعرف...؟
Do you know whether...?	*Hal ta'rif idhaa kaana...?* هل تعرف إذا كان...؟
Do you have...?	*Hal ladaykum...?* هل لديكم...؟

Do you have a vegetarian dish, please?	*Hal ladayka tabaq khudrawaat min fadlik?* هل لديك طبق خضروات من فضلك؟
I would like...	*Uriidu...* أريد...
I'd like a kilo of apples, please	*Uriidu kiilu tuffaah min fadlik* أريد كيلو تفاح من فضلك
May I?	*Hal yumkinuni an?* هل يمكنني أن؟
May I take this away?	*Hal yumkin an asluka haadhaa attariiq?* هل يمكن أن أسلك هذ الطريق؟
Can I smoke here?	*Hal yumkin an udakhina hunaa?* هل يمكن أن أدخن هنا؟
Could I ask you a question?	*Hal yumkin an as'alaka su'aalan?* هل يمكن أن أسألك سؤالا؟

2.3 How to reply

Yes, of course	*Na'am, tab'an* نعم، طبعا
Sure	*Akiid* أكيد
No, I'm sorry	*Laa, anaa aasif* لا، أنا آسف
Yes, what can I do for you?	*Na'am, hal min khidma uqaddimuhaa laka?* نعم، هل من خدمة أقدمها لك؟
Just a moment, please	*Lahza min fadlik* لحظة، من فضلك

No, I don't have time now	*Kallaa, laysa ladayya al-waqtu al-aan* كلا ، ليس لدي الوقت الآن
No, that's impossible	*Laa, haadhaa mustahiil* لا ، هذا مستحيل
I think so/I think that's absolutely right	*Azun kadhaalik/azunnu dhaalika sahihan qat'an* أظن كذلك/أظن ذلك صحيحا قطعا
I agree/I don't agree	*Anaa uwaafiq/laa uwaafiq* انا أوافق/لا أوافق
I hope so too	*Atamannaa an yakuuna kadhaalik* أتمنى أن يكون كذلك
No, not at all/ Absolutely not	*Laa, laysa kadhaalik/qat'an laa* لا ، ليس كذلك/قطعا لا
No, no one	*Laa, laa ahad* لا ، لا أحد
No, nothing	*Laa, laa shay'* لا ، لا شيء
That's right	*Haadhaa sahiih* هذا صحيح
Something's wrong	*Hunaaka mushkila maa* هناك مشكلة ما
OK/it's fine	*Na'am/haadhaa jayyid* نعم/هذا جيد
All right	*Tamaam* تمام
Perhaps	*Rubbamaa* ربما
I don't know	*Laa a'rif* لا أعرف

2.4 Thank you

Thank you	*Shukran* شكرا
You're welcome	*Ahlan wa sahlan bika* أهلا وسهلا بك
Thank you very much/ Many thanks	*Shukran kathiiran/jaziilu kathiiran* شكرا كثيرا/جزيل كثيرا
No problem	*Laa mushkila* لا مشكلة ،
Very kind of you	*Hadhaa lutfun minka* هذا لطف منك
My pleasure	*Bikulli suruur* بكل سرور
I enjoyed it very much	*Istamta'tu bidhaalika kathiiran* استمتعت بذلك كثيرا
Thank you for...	*Shukran laka 'alaa...* شكرا لك على...
You shouldn't have/ That was so kind of you	*Lam yakun yalzamuk/kaana dhaalika lutfan minka* لم يكن يلزمك/كان ذلك لطفا منك
Don't mention it!	*Al-'afw* العفو
That's all right	*Laysat mushkila* ليست مشكلة

2.5 I'm sorry

Excuse me/pardon me/ sorry	*'Afwan/arjuu al-ma'dhira/aasif* عفوا/أرجو المعذرة/آسف

Sorry, I didn't know that...	*'Afwan lam akun a'rifu annahu...* عفوا لم أكن أعرف أنه...
I do apologize	*Anaa a'tadhir* أنا أعتذر
I'm sorry	*Anaa aasif* أنا آسف
I didn't mean it/it was an accident	*Lam akun aqsid dhaalik/lam takun maqsoodah* لم أكن أقصد ذلك/لم تكن مقصودة
That's all right/don't worry about it	*Kullu shay' tamaam/laa tahtam* كل شيء تمام/لا تهتم
Never mind/forget it	*Laa tahtam/insa dhaalik* لا تهتم/انس ذلك

2.6 What do you think?

What do you prefer/ like best?	*Maadhaa tufaddil/tuhib akthar?* ماذا تفضل؟/تحب أكثر؟
What do you think?	*Maa ra'yuka?* ما رأيك؟
Don't you like dancing?	*Alaa tuhib an taqus?* ألا تحب أن ترقص؟
I don't mind	*Laa yahum* لا يهم
Well done!	*Ahsanta sun'an!* أحسنت صنعا
Not bad!	*Laa ba'sa!* لا بأس
Great/marvelous!	*'Aziim/raa'i'!* عظيم/رائع

Wonderful!	*Raa'i'!* رائع
How lovely!	*Kam haadhaa jamiil!* كم هذا جميل
I am pleased for you	*Anaa masrur bi-sha'nika* انا مسرور بشأنك
I'm (not) very happy/ delighted to...	*Anaa (ghayr) masruur jiddan/* *mubtahij li...* أنا (غير) مسرور جدا/مبتهج ل...
It's really nice here!	*Innahu haqqan makaanun jamiil!* إنه حقا مكان جميل
How nice!	*Kam haadhaa jamiil!* كم هذا جميل
How nice for you!	*Haadhaa amrun raa'i' bin-nisbati laka!* هذا امر رائع بالنسبة لك
I'm very happy with...	*Anaa lastu sa'iidan jiddan bi...* أنا لست سعيدا جدا ب...
I'm glad that...	*Anaa masruurun annahu...* أنا مسرور انه...
I'm having a great time	*Innanii atasallaa kathiiran* انني أتسلى كثيرا

I can't wait till tomorrow/
  I'm looking forward to
  tomorrow
	Laa astatii' an antazir ilaa al-ghad/
	atattala' ilaa al-ghad
	لا أستطيع أن أنتظر الى الغد/
	أتطلع الى الغد

I hope it works out	*Atamanna an tasiira al'umuuru* *kamaa yajibu* أتمنى أن تسير الأمور كما يجب
How awful!	*Yaa lahu min amrin kariih* يا له من أمر كريه

English	Arabic (transliteration / script)
It's horrible!	*Innahu amrun fazii'!* إنه أمر فظيع
That's ridiculous!	*Haadhaa amrun sakhiif!* هذا أمر سخيف
That's terrible!	*Yaa lahu min amrin rahiib!* يا له من أمر رهيب
What a pity/shame!	*Yaa lash-shafaqa/yaa lal'asaf!* يا للشفقة/يا للأسف
How disgusting!	*Yaa lahu min amrin muz'ij!* يا له من أمر مزعج
What nonsense/how silly!	*Ayya huraa' haadhaa/yaa lahu min sukhf!* أي هراء هذا/يا له من سخف
I am completely exhausted (m/f)	*Anaa munhak/munhaka jiddan* أنا منهك/منهكة جدا
I am excited (m/f) to...	*Anaa mutahammis/mutahammisa* أنا متحمس/متحمسة لـ ...
I am looking forward to...	*Atatalla'u ilaa...* أتطلع إلى...
I'm bored to death	*Ash'ur bi-malal shadiid* أشعر بملل شديد
I'm fed up	*Anaa munza'ij* أنا منزعج
This is no good	*Haadhaa laysa jayyidan* هذا ليس جيدا
This is not what I expected	*Laysa haadhaa maa tawaqqa't* ليس هذا ما توقعت

3 Small Talk

3. Small Talk

3.1 Introductions

May I introduce myself?	*Ismah lii an uqaddima nafsii?* اسمح لي أن أقدم نفسي؟
My name's...	*Ismii...* اسمي...
I'm...	*Anaa...* أنا...
What's your name? (formal/informal)	*Maa ismuk?/maa ismu hadratik?* ما اسمك؟/ما اسم حضرتك؟
May I introduce...?	*Ismah lii an uqaddima laka...?* إسمح لي ان اقدم لك...؟
This is my wife/husband	*Haadhihi zawjatii/haadhaa zawjii* هذه زوجتي/هذا زوجي
This is my daughter/son	*Haadhihi ibnatii/haadhaa ibnii* هذه ابنتي/هذا ابني
This is my mother (mom)/ father (dad)	*Haadhaa waalidii (abii)/haadhihi ummii (waalidatii)* هذه أمي (والدتي)/هذا والدي (أبي)
This is my fiancée/fiancé	*Haadhihi khatiibatii/haadhaa khatiibii* هذه خطيبتي/هذا خطيبي
This is my friend (f/m)	*Haadhaa sadiiqii/haadhihi sadiiqatii* هذا صديقي/هذه صديقتي
How do you do?	*Kayfa haaluk?* كيف حالك؟
I am fine, praise God	*Anaa bikhair, al-hamdu lillah* أنا بخير ، الحمد لله

Hi, nice to meet you (informal)	*Ahlan, masruur liliqaa'ik* أهلا، مسرور للقائك
Pleased to meet you (formal)	*Anaa sa'iid bi-liqaa'ik* أنا سعيد بلقائك
Where are you from?	*Min aina anta?* من أين أنت؟
I'm American	*Anaa amariikiyy* أنا أمريكي
I am from America	*Anaa min amrika* أنا من أمريكا
I am not Canadian	*Anaa lastu kanadiyan* أنا لست كنديا
What city do you live in?	*Fii ayyati madiinatin taskun?* في أي مدينة تسكن؟
In...near...	*fii...qurb...* في...قرب...
Have you been here long?	*Hal ji'ta mundhu waqtin tawiilin?* هل جئت منذ وقت طويل؟
A few days	*Bid'at ayyaam* بضعة أيام
How long are you staying here?	*Kam satuqiim (satabqaa) hunaa?* كم ستقيم (ستبقى) هنا؟
We're probably leaving tomorrow/in two weeks	*Muhtamal an nughadir ghadan/ba'da usbuu'ayn* محتمل ان نغادر غدا/بعد اسبوعين
Where are you (m/f) staying?	*Ayna tuqiim/tuqiimiin?* أين تقيم/تقيمين؟
I'm staying in a hotel/ an apartment	*Uqiimu fii funduq/shaqqa* أقيم في فندق/شقة

At a campsite	*Fii mukhayyam* في مخيم
I'm staying with friends/ relatives	*Uqiimu ma'a asdiqaa'/aqaarib* أقيم مع أصدقاء/أقارب
Are you here alone?/ with your family?	*Hal anta huna wahdak/ma'a 'aa'ilatik?* هل أنت هنا وحدك؟/مع عائلتك؟
I'm alone	*Anaa wahdii* أنا وحدي
I'm with my partner/ wife/husband	*Anaa ma'a rafiiqii (qariinii)/zawjatii/ zawjii* انا مع رفيقي (قريني)/زوجتي/زوجي
– with my family	*ma'a 'aa'ilatii* مع عائلتي
– with my relatives	*ma'a aqaaribii* مع أقاربي
– with a friend/friends	*ma'a sadiiq/asdiqaa'* مع صديق/أصدقاء
Are you married? (m/f)	*Hal anta mutazawwij/anti mutazawwija?* هل أنت متزوج/متزوجة؟
Are you engaged?	*Hal anti makhtuuba?* هل انت مخطوبة؟
Do you have a steady boyfriend/girlfriend?	*Hal laki sadiiq thaabit/sadiika thaabita?* هل لك صديق ثابت/صديقة ثابتة؟
That's none of your business	*Haadhaa al-amr laa yakhusuk* هذا الامر لا يخصلك
I'm married (m/f)	*Anaa mutazawwij/mutazawwija* أنا متزوج/متزوجة
I'm single (m)	*Anaa a'zab* أنا أعزب

I'm not married (m/f)	*Anaa lastu mutazawwij/mutazawwija* أنا لست متزوجا/متزوجة
I'm separated (m/f)	*Anaa munfasil/munfasila* أنا منفصل/أنا منفصلة
I'm divorced (m/f)	*Anaa mutallaq/mutallaqa* أنا مطلق/مطلقة
I'm a widow/widower	*Anaa armala/armal* أنا أرمل/أرملة
I live alone/with someone	*Ana askun wahdii/ma'a shakhsin maa* أنا أسكن وحدي/مع شخص ما
Do you have any children/ grandchildren?	*Hal ladayka ayya atfaal/ahfaad?* هل لديك أي أطفال/أحفاد؟
How old are you?	*Kam 'umruk?* كم عمرك؟
I'm...(years old)	*'Umrii...* عمري...
How old is she/he?	*Kam 'umruhaa/'umruhu?* كم عمرها/عمره؟
She's/he's...(years old)	*'Umruhaa/'umruhu...* عمرها/عمره...
What do you do for a living?	*Maadhaa ta'mal?* ماذا تعمل؟
I am a teacher (m/f)	*Anaa mu'allim/mu'allima* أنا معلم/معلمة
I work in an office	*A'mal fii maktab (daa'ira)* أعمل في مكتب (دائرة)
I'm a student (m/f)	*Anaa taalib/taaliba* انا طالب/طالبة
I'm unemployed (m/f)	*Laa a'mal ('aatil/'aatila 'an al-'amal)* لا اعمل (عاطل/عاطلة عن العمل)

I'm retired (m/f)	*Anaa mutaqaa'id/mutaqaa'ida* أنا متقاعد/متقاعدة
I'm a housewife	*Anaa rabbatu bayt* أنا ربة بيت
Do you like your job?	*Hal tuhibbu 'amalak?* هل تحب عملك؟
Yes, I like my job	*Na'am, anaa uhibbu 'amalii* نعم ، أنا أحب عملي
No, it is a hard job	*Laa, innahu shaaq* لا ، إنه عمل شاق
Mostly I do, but I prefer vacations	*Na'am ghaaliban, laakin ufadil al-'ijaazaat* نعم غالبا ، لكن أفضل الإجازات

3.2 I beg your pardon?

I don't speak any Arabic/ I speak a little Arabic	*Anaa laa atakallamu al-'arabiyya kathiiran/anaa atakallamu al-'arabiyya qaliilan* انا لا أتكلم العربية كثيرا/انا أتكلم العربية قليلا
I'm American (m/f)	*Anaa amariikiy/amariikiyya* أنا أمريكي/أمريكية
Do you speak English?	*Hal tatakallamu al-inkiliiziyah?* هل تتكلم الانكليزية؟
Is there anyone who speaks...?	*Hal yuujad man yatakallmu al...?* هل يوجد من يتكلم ال...؟
I beg your pardon/what?	*'Afwan maadhaa qulta/maadhaa?* عفوا ماذا قلت/ماذا؟
I don't understand	*Lam afham* لم أفهم

Do you understand me?	*Hal tafhamunii?* هل تفهمني؟
Could you repeat that, please?	*Hal yumkin an tu'iid maa qulta, min fadlik?* هل يمكن أن تعيد ما قلت، من فضلك؟
Could you speak more slowly, please?	*Hal yumkin an tatakallama bi-but'in min fadlik?* هل يمكن أن تتكلم ببطء من فضلك؟
What does that/that word mean?	*Maadhaa ya'nii dhaalik/maadhaa ta'nii tilka al-kalimah?* ماذا يعني ذلك/ماذا تعني تلك الكلمة؟
It's more or less the same as...	*Hiya taqriiban nafsu ma'na kalimat...* هي تقريبا نفس معنى كلمة...
Could you write that down for me, please?	*Hal yumkin an taktuba lii dhaalik min fadlik?* هل يمكن أن تكتب لي ذلك من فضلك؟
Could you spell that for me, please?	*Hal yumkin an tatahajjaa lii dhaalik min fadlik?* هل يمكن أن تتهجى لي ذلك من فضلك؟

(See 1.9 Telephone alphabets)

Could you point that out in this phrase book, please?	*Hal yumkin an tushiira ilaa dhaalik fil-kitaab, min fadlik?* هل يمكن أن تشير إلى ذلك في الكتاب، من فضلك؟
Just a minute, I'll look it up	*Daqiiqa wahida, sawfa abhathu 'an dhaalik* دقيقة واحدة، سوف أبحث عن ذلك
I can't find the word/the sentence	*Laa astatii'u an ajida haadhihi al-kalima/al-jumla* لا أستطيع أن أجد هذه الكلمة/الجملة

How do you say that in...?	*Kayfa taquul <u>dh</u>aalika fii al-lu<u>gh</u>a...?* كيف تقول ذلك في اللغة...؟
How do you pronounce that?	*Kayfa talfa<u>z</u> <u>dh</u>aalika?* كيف تلفظ ذلك؟

3.3 Starting/ending a conversation

Excuse me (formal/informal)	*U'<u>dh</u>rnii/arjuu al-ma'<u>dh</u>ira* اعذرني/أرجو المعذرة
Could I ask you something? (formal/informal)	*Hal yumkin an as'alaka <u>sh</u>ay'an/ladayya su'aal?* هل يمكن أن أسألك شيئا/لدي سؤال؟
Could you help me, please?	*Hal tasta<u>t</u>ii'u an tusaa'idanii min fa<u>d</u>lik?* هل تستطيع أن تساعدني من فضلك؟
Yes, what's the problem?	*Na'am, maa l-mu<u>sh</u>kila?* نعم، ما المشكلة؟
What can I do for you?	*Kayfa yumkin an usaa'idaka?* كيف يمكن أن أساعدك؟
Sorry, I don't have time now	*'Afwan, laysa ladayya waqtun al'aan* عفوا، ليس لدي وقت الآن
Do you have a light?	*Hal ladayka qaddaa<u>h</u>a?* هل لديك قداحة؟
May I join you?	*Hal yumkin an an<u>d</u>amma ilaykum?* هل يمكن أن أنضم إليكم؟
Could you take a picture of me/us?	*Hal yumkin an ta'<u>kh</u>u<u>dh</u>a lii/lanaa suura?* هل يمكن أن تأخذ لي/لنا صورة؟
Leave me alone! (formal/informal)	*Arjuuk an tatrukanii lihaalii/utruknii liwa<u>h</u>dii!* أرجوك أن تتركني لحالي/اتركني لوحدي

Get lost! (formal/informal)	*Insarif 'annii/arjuuka an tadhhaba min hunaa!*
	انصرف عني/ارجوك أن تذهب من هنا
Go away or I'll scream	*Ib'id 'annii wa illaa sa-asrukh*
	ابعد عني والا سأصرخ

3.4 A chat about the weather

See also 1.5 The weather

It's so hot/cold today!	*Al-yawm at-taqs haar/baarid jiddan!*
	اليوم الطقس حار/بارد جدا
Isn't it a lovely day?	*Alaysa al-yawm jamiil?*
	أليس اليوم جميلا؟
It's so windy/what a storm!	*Hawaa'un shadiid/ya lahaa min 'aasifa!*
	هواء شديد/يالها من عاصفة
All that rain/snow!	*Kullu haadhaa al-matar/ath-thalj!*
	كل هذا المطر/الثلج!
It's so foggy!	*Dabaab shadiid!*
	ضباب شديد!
Has the weather been like this for long?	*Hal kaana t-taqsu haakadhaa mundhu waqt tawiil?*
	هل كان الطقس هكذا منذ وقت طويل؟
Is it always this hot/cold here?	*At-taqsu hunaa daa'iman haar/baarid?*
	الطقس هنا دائما حار/بارد؟
Is it always this dry/ humid here?	*At-taqsu hunaa daa'iman jaaf/ratib?*
	الطقس هنا دائما جاف/رطب؟

3.5 Hobbies

| Do you have any hobbies? | *Hal ladyka ayyat hiwaayaat?* |
| | هل لديك أية هوايات؟ |

I like video games	*Uhibbu al'aab al-fidyo*
	أحب ألعاب الفيديو
I like karaoke	*Uhibbu al-karawki*
	أحب الكاراوكي
I enjoy listening to music	*Anaa uhibbu al-istimaa'a ilaa almuusiiqaa*
	أنا أحب الاستماع الى الموسيقي
I like card games	*Uhibbu li'bat al-waraq*
	أحب لعبة الورق
I like the cinema	*Uhibbu as-siinamaa*
	أحب السينما
I like sailing	*Uhibbu ar-rahalaat al-bahariya*
	أحب الرحلات البحرية
I like running/jogging	*Uhibbu ar-rakd/al-'adw*
	أحب الركض/العدو

3.6 Invitations

Are you doing anything tonight?	*Hal anta mashghuul al-layla?*
	هل انت مشغول الليلة؟
Do you have any plans for today/this afternoon/tonight?	*Hal ladyaka barnaamaj lihaadhaa al-yawm/al-yawm ba'da z-zuhr/allayla?*
	هل لديك برنامج لهذا اليوم/اليوم بعد الظهر/الليلة؟
Would you like to go out with me?	*Hal tuhib an nakhruja sawiyyatan?*
	هل تحب ان نخرج سوية؟
Would you like to go dancing with me?	*Hal tuhib an nadhhaba ilaa r-raqsi?*
	هل تحب ان نذهب إلى الرقص؟
Would you like to have lunch/dinner with me?	*Hal tuhib an ta'tiya ma'ii lilghadaa'/lil'ashaa'?*
	هل تحب ان تأتي معي للغداء/للعشاء؟

Would you like to come to the beach with me?	*Hal tuhib an ta'tiya ma'ii ilaa sh-shaati'?*
	هل تحب ان تأتي معي إلى الشاطئ؟
Would you like to come into town with us?	*Hal tuhib an ta'tiya ma'anaa ilaa l-madiina?*
	هل تحب ان تاتي معنا الى المدينة؟
Will you go to the movie theater with me?	*Hal saufa tadhhab ma'ii ilaa as-sinimaa?*
	هل سوف تذهب معي إلى السينما ؟
Do you like comedy movies?	*Hal tuhibbu al-aflaam al-kumiidiya?*
	هل تحب الأفلام الكوميدية؟
– romantic movies	*aflaam rumansiya*
	أفلام رومانسية
– action movies	*aflaam al-haraka*
	أفلام الحركة
I like science fiction movies	*Uhibbu aflaam al-khayaal al'ilmii*
	أحب أفلام الخيال العلمي
I do not like historical films	*Laa uhibbu al-aflaam at-taariikhiya*
	لا أحب الأفلام التاريخية
Would you like to come and see some friends with us?	*Hal tuhib an ta'tiya ma'anaa liziyaarat ba'd l-asdiqaa'?*
	هل تحب ان تأتي معنا لزيارة بعض الاصدقاء؟
Shall we dance?	*Hal tuhib an narqusa?*
	هل تحب أن نرقص؟
– sit at the bar?	*Hal najlis fii l-baar?*
	هل نجلس في البار؟
– get something to drink?	*Hal turiid mashruuban maa?*
	هل تريد مشروبا ما؟
Shall we go for a walk/ drive?	*Hal turiid an natamashaa (natajawwal bi s-sayyaara)?*
	هل تريد أن نتمشى (نتجول بالسيارة) ؟

Yes, all right	*Na'm, haadhaa jayyid* نعم، هذا جيد
Good idea	*Fikra jayyida* فكرة جيدة
No thank you	*Laa shukran* لا شكرا
Maybe later	*Rubbamaa fiimaa ba'd* ربما فيما بعد
I don't feel like it	*Laa ash'ur biraghbatin fii* لا اشعر برغبة في
I don't have time	*Laysa ladyya waqt* ليس لدي وقت
I already have a date	*Anaa ladayya maw'id* انا لدي موعد
I'm not very good at dancing/volleyball/ swimming	*Anaa laa ujiidu ar-raqs/al-kurat at-taa'ira/as-sibaaha* انا لا أجيد الرقص/كرة الطائرة/السباحة

3.7 Paying a compliment

You're beautiful/you're handsome	*Anti jamiila/anta wasiim* أنت جميلة/أنت وسيم
I like your car!	*Sayyaaratuka tu'jibunii!* سيارتك تعجبني
I like your ski outfit!	*Tu'jibunii libaasu t-tazalluji ladayka!* تعجبني لباس التزلج لديك
You are very nice (m/f)	*Anta latiif/anti latiifa* أنت لطيف/أنت لطيفة
What a good boy/girl!	*Haqqan innahu walad mumtaaz/bint mumtaaza!* حقا إنه ولد ممتاز/بنت ممتازة

You're a good dancer (m/f)	*Anta raaqis jayyid/anti raaqisa jayyida* أنت راقص جيد/أنت راقصة جيدة
You're a very good cook	*Anta tabbaakh jayyid jiddan* أنت طباخ جيد جدا
You're a good soccer player	*Antaa laa'ib kurat qadam maahir* أنت لاعب كرة قدم ماهر

3.8 Intimate comments/questions

I like being with you	*Uhibbu an akuuna ma'ak* احب ان اكون معك
I've missed you so much	*Anaa mushtaaqun ilayk* انا مشتاق اليك
I dreamt about you (m/f)	*Halimtu bika/biki* حلمت بك
I think about you all day	*Anaa ufakkiru fiiki ṯuul al-yawm* انا افكر فيك طول اليوم
I've been thinking about you all day	*Kuntu ufakkiru fiiki ṯuul al-yawm* كنت افكر فيك طول اليوم
You have such a sweet smile	*Ladayki ibtisaama jamiila* لديك ابتسامة جميلة
You have such beautiful eyes	*'Uyuunuki jamiila* عيونك جميلة
I'm fond of you (m/f)	*Anaa mughram/mughrama bik* انا مغرم/مغرمة بك
I love you	*Anaa uhibbuk* أنا أحبك
I love you too	*Anaa uhibbuk aydan* أنا أحبك ايضا

I'm in love with you	*Anaa waqa'tu fii ḥubbik* أنا وقعت في حبك
I'm in love with you too	*Anaa aydan waq'atu fii ḥubbik* أنا ايضا وقعت في حبك
I don't feel as strongly about you	*Mashaa'irii tujaahak laysat qawiyyatan* مشاعري تجاهك ليست قوية
I already have a girlfriend/boyfriend	*Anaa ladyya ṣadiiqa/ṣadiiq* انا لدي صديقة/صديق
I'm not ready for that	*Lastu musta'iddan lidhaalik* لست مستعدا لذلك
I don't want to rush into it	*Laa uriidu an akuuna musta'jilan fii dhaalik* لا اريد ان اكون مستعجلا في ذلك
Take your hands off me	*Irfa' yadaka 'annii* ارفع يدك عني
Okay, no problem	*Tayyib laysat hunaaka mushkila* طيب ليست هناك مشكلة
Will you spend the night with me?	*Hal taqddiina al-layla ma'ii?* هل تقضين الليلة معي؟
I'd like to go to bed with you	*Uḥibbu an anaama ma'aki* احب أن انام معك
Only if we use a condom	*Faqat idhaa istakhdamnaa al-ghilaaf al-mattaatii (al-kabuut)* فقط اذا استخدمنا الغلاف المطاطي (الكبوت)
We have to be careful about AIDS	*Yajib an nakuuna ḥadhiriin mina al-aydiz* يجب ان نكون حذرين من الايدز
That's what they all say	*Haadhaa maa yaquluhu al-jamii'* هذا ما يقوله الجميع

We shouldn't take
 any risks

Yajibu an laa nujaazif

يجب ان لا نجازف

Do you have a condom?

Hal ladayka al-ghilaaf al-mattatii?

هل لديك الغلاف المطاطي (الكبوت) ؟

No? Then the answer's no

Laa? Idhan al-jawaab laa

لا؟ اذن الجواب لا

3.9 Congratulations and condolences

Happy birthday/many
 happy returns/happy
 name day

*'Lid miilaad sa'iid/'Umr tawiil/Yawm
sa'iid*

عيد ميلاد سعيد/عمر طويل/يوم سعيد

Please accept my
 condolences

Ta'aaziina

تعازينا

My deepest sympathy

Ma'a akhlas mashaa'irinaa

مع أخلص مشاعرنا

3.10 Arrangements

When will I see you again?

Mataa sa-araaka marratan ukhraa?

متى سأراك مرة اخرى؟

Are you free over the
 weekend?

*Hal ladayk waqtun khilaal 'utlat
nihaayat al-usbuu'?*

هل لديك وقت خلال عطلة نهاية الاسبوع؟

What's the plan, then?

Maa al-khutta (al-barnaamaj) idhan?

ما الخطة (البرنامج) اذن؟

Where shall we meet?

Ayna sanaltaqii?

اين سنلتقي؟

Shall I pick you up?

*Hal turiidunii an as-habaka ma'ii fii
as-sayyaara?*

هل تريدني ان اصحبك معي في السيارة؟

I have to be home by...	*Yajibu an akuuna fii al-bayt as-saa'a...*
	...يجب ان اكون في البيت الساعة
I don't want to see you anymore	*Laa uriidu an araaka marratan ukhraa abadan*
	لا اريد ان اراك مرة اخرى ابدا

3.11 Being the host(ess)

See also 4 Eating out

Can I offer you a drink? (formal/informal)	*Hal triidu mashruban?*
	هل تريد مشروبا ؟
What would you like to drink? (formal/informal)	*Maadhaa tuhib an tashrab?*
	ماذا تحب ان تشرب؟
Something non-alcoholic, please	*Ayya shay'in ghayr al-kuhuul min fadlik*
	أي شيء غير الكحول من فضلك
Do you prefer a cold or hot drink?	*Hal tufaddil mashruuban baaridan am saakhinan*
	هل تفضل مشروبا باردا أم ساخنا ؟
Would you like a cigarette?	*Hal turiid siijaara?*
	هل تريد سيجارة؟
I don't smoke	*Anaa laa udakhin*
	انا لا ادخن
Would you like some sweets?	*Hal tuhibbu ba'd al-halwaa*
	هل تحب بعض الحلوى؟

3.12 Saying good-bye

Can I take you home?	*Hal turiidu an astahibaka ilaa al-bayt?*
	هل تريد ان اصطحبك إلى البيت؟
Can I write/call you?	*Hal yumkin an uraasilak/attasil bik?*
	هل يمكن ان اراسلك/اتصل بك؟

Will you write to me/ call me?	*Hal sa-turaasilunii/tatta<u>s</u>il bii?*
	هل ستراسلني/تتصل بي؟
Can I have your address/ phone number?	*Hal yumkin an tu'tiyanii 'unwaanak/ raqam haatifik?*
	هل يمكن ان تعطيني عنوانك/رقم هاتفك؟
Thanks for everything	*<u>Sh</u>ukran 'alaa kulli <u>sh</u>ay'*
	شكرا على كل شيئ
It was a lot of fun	*Kaanat mumti'a*
	كانت ممتعة
Say hello to…	*Balli<u>gh</u> ta<u>h</u>iyyaatii li…*
	بلغ تحياتي لـ...
All the best	*Atamanna laka kulla al<u>kh</u>ayr*
	اتمنى لك كل الخير
Good luck	*<u>H</u>a<u>zz</u>an sa'iidan*
	حظا سعيدا
When will you be back?	*Mataa sata'uud?*
	متى ستعود؟
I'll be waiting for you	*Sawfa akuun binti<u>z</u>aarik*
	سوف اكون بانتظارك
I'd like to see you again	*U<u>h</u>ibbu an araaka marratan u<u>kh</u>raa*
	احب ان اراك مرة اخرى
I hope we meet again soon	*Atamannaa an naltaqii marratan u<u>kh</u>raa qariiban*
	أتمنى ان نلتقي مرة اخرى قريبا
Here's our address. If you're ever in the United States…	*Haa<u>dh</u>aa 'unwaanunaa, i<u>dh</u>aa saadafa an zurta amariika…*
	هذا عنواننا إذا صادف أن زرت امريكا...
You'd be more than welcome	*Nura<u>hh</u>ibu bika daa'iman*
	نرحب بك دائما

4 Eating out

4. Eating out

Mealtimes

The Middle East is an ecologically diverse area, so it is important to remember that as such most societies conduct their lives in ways that reflect their environment as well as their specific social and cultural heritage. Nevertheless, eating is one of the common cultural practices in most countries of the Middle East where people usually not only eat but celebrate life through eating. Each meal is a family occasion and guests (including strangers) are warmly invited to share whatever is prepared. Like other countries, the three main meals are:

1. **fatour as-sabaah** (breakfast), eaten sometime between 7.30 and 9.00 a.m. It generally consists of bread, eggs, olives and tea. In the Arab countries of North Africa, croissant, toast (with butter, honey and jam) and milk coffee are also common.

2. **ghadaa'** (lunch), traditionally eaten at home between 12.00 and 1.30 p.m., includes pickles, salads, breads/rice and a hot (meat) dish.

3. **ashaa'** (dinner), at around 7.00 or 8.00 p.m., is a light meal, often including salad, soup and sometimes leftovers from the main lunch.

In restaurants

Most restaurants have a cover charge which includes bread, pickled vegetables, olives and dips. In most countries, no specific service charge is required.

At the restaurant

I'd like to reserve a table for seven o'clock, please	*Uriidu an aḥjiza ṯaawila assaa'a assaabi'ah min faḏlik* أريد ان احجز طاولة الساعة السابعة من فضلك

هل لديك حجز؟	Do you have a reservation?
الاسم من فضلك؟	What name, please?
تفضل من هنا	This way, please
هذه الطاولة محجوزة	This table is reserved
سوف تتوفر طاولة بعد خمسة عشرة دقيقة	We'll have a table free in fifteen minutes
لو سمحت ممكن ان تنتظر؟	Would you mind waiting?

A table for two, please	*Taawila li shakhsayn (li nafarayn) min fadlik* طاولة لشخصين/لنفرين من فضلك
We've not reserved	*Lam nahjiz* لم نحجز
Is the restaurant open yet?	*hal mazaala al-mat'am maftuuhan?* هل ما زال المطعم مفتوحا؟
What time does the restaurant open?/ What time does the restaurant close?	*Mataa yaftah al-mat'am?/mataa yughliq al-mat'am?* متى يفتح المطعم؟/متى يغلق المطعم؟
Can we wait for a table?	*Hal yumkin an nantazir lihiin tawaffur taawila?* هل يمكن ان ننتظر لحين توفر طاولة؟
Do we have to wait long?	*Hal sa-nantazir tawiilan?* هل سننتظر طويلا؟
Is this seat taken?	*Hal haadhaa al-maq'ad mahjuuz?* هل هذا المقعد محجوز؟
Could we sit here/there?	*Hal yumkin an najlisa hunaa/hunaak?* هل يمكن ان نجلس هنا/هناك؟

Can we sit by the window?	*Hal yumkin an najlisa bijaanib ash-shubbaak?*
	هل يمكن ان نجلس بجانب الشباك؟
Are there any tables outside?	*Hal tuujad ṭaawilaat fil-khaarij?*
	هل توجد طاولات في الخارج؟
Do you have another chair for us?	*Hal ladayka kursiy aakhar?*
	هل لديك كرسي اخر؟
Do you have a highchair?	*Hal ladayka kursiy aṭfaal?*
	هل لديك كرسي أطفال؟
Is there a socket for this bottle-warmer?	*Hal yuujad miqbas li-musakhin az-zujajat haadha?*
	هل يوجد مقبس لمسخن الزجاجات هذا؟
Could you warm up this bottle?	*Hal yumkin an tusakhin haadhi az-zujaja?*
	هل يمكن أن تسخن هذه الزجاجة؟
Not too hot, please	*Laysa haaran jiddan min faḍlik*
	ليس حارا جدا من فضلك
Is there somewhere I can change the baby's diaper?	*Ayna yumkin an ughayira haffaada aṭ-ṭifl?*
	اين يمكن ان اغير حفاضة الطفل؟
Where is the restroom?	*Ayna al-hammam?*
	أين الحمام؟

4.2 Ordering

Waiter/Waitress!	*Ayyuhaa an-naadil/an-naadila*
	أيها النادل/النادلة
Madam!	*Sayidatii*
	سيدتي
Sir	*Sayidii*
	سيدي

We'd like something to eat/drink	*Nuriid shai'an na'kul/nashrab* نريد شيئا نأكل/نشرب
Could I have a quick meal?	*Hal yumkin an ahsula 'alaa wajba sarii'a?* هل يمكن ان احصل على وجبة سريعة
We don't have much time	*Laysa ladainaa al-kathiir mina al-waqt* ليس لدينا الكثير من الوقت
We'd like to have a drink first	*Awwalan nuriidu an nashraba* اولا نريد ان نشرب
Could we see the menu/ wine list, please?	*Hal yumkin an nattali'a 'alaa qaa'imat al-ma'kuulaat/al-mashruubaat min fadlik?* هل يمكن ان نطلع على قائمة الماكولات/ المشروبات من فضلك؟
Do you have a menu in English?	*Hal ladayka qaa'imat ma'kuulaat bil-lugha al-inkliziya?* هل لديكم قائمة مأكولات باللغة الإنكليزية؟
Do you have a dish of the day/a tourist menu?	*Hal ladaykum tabaq al-yawm/ qaa'imat ta'aam as-saa'ih?* هل لديكم طبق اليوم/قائمة طعام السائح؟
We haven't made a choice yet	*Lam nuqarrir ba'du* لم نقرر بعد
What do you recommend?	*Bi-maadhaa tansah?* بماذا تنصح؟
What are the local specialities?	*Maa hiya al-atbaaq al-mahalliya ladaykum?* ما هي الأطباق المحلية لديكم؟
I like strawberries/olives	*Uriidu faraawla/zaytuun* اريد فراولة/زيتون
I don't like meat/fish	*Laa uhibbu al-lahma/as-samaka* لا أحب اللحم/السمك

What's this?	*Maa haadhaa?* ما هذا؟
Does it have...in it?	*Hal yuujad ...fiihi?* هل يوجد...فيه؟
Is it stuffed with...?	*Hal haadhaa mahshuu bi...?* هل هذا محشو ب...؟
What does it taste like?	*Maa ta'muhu?* ما طعمه؟
Is this a hot or a cold dish?	*Hal haadhaa tabaq haar am baarid?* هل هذا طبق حار ام بارد؟
Is this sweet?	*Hal haadhaa hulw?* هل هذا حلو؟
Is this hot (spicy)?	*Hal haadhaa haar (fiihi fulful haar)?* هل هذا حار (فيه فلفل حار)؟
Do you have anything else, by any chance?	*Hal ladaykum ay shay' aakhar?* هل لديكم اي شيء اخر؟
I'm on a salt-free diet	*Anaa uriid ta'aaman khaaliyan min al-milh* انا اريد طعاما خاليا من الملح

ماذا تطلب؟	What would you like?
هل قررتم؟	Have you decided?
هل ترغبون بالشراب اولا؟	Would you like a drink first?
ماذا تحبون أن تشربوا اولا؟	What would you like to drink?
لم يبق لدينا...	We've run out of...
وجبة شهية	Enjoy your meal
هل كل شيء على ما يرام؟	Is everything all right?
هل يمكن ان انظف الطاولة؟	May I clear the table?

I can't eat pork	*Anaa laa aakulu lahma l-khanziir* انا لا اكل لحم الخنزير
I can't have sugar	*Anaa laa asstatii'u an aakhudha assukkar* انا لا استطيع ان آخذ السكر
I'm on a fat-free diet	*Uriid ta'aaman khaaliyan min ad-dassim* اريد طعاما خاليا من الدسم
I can't have spicy food	*Laa asstatii'u an atanaawala ta'aaman fiihi fulful haar* لا استطيع ان اتناول طعاما فيه فلفل حار
We'll have what those people are having	*Nuriid nafs tabaq 'ulaa'ika an-naas* نريد نفس طبق اولئك الناس
I'd like...	*Arghabu fii...* ارغب في...
We're not having a rice dish	*Laysa ladaynaa tabaq al-aruz* ليس لدينا طبق الارز
Could I have some more bread, please?	*Hal yumkin an ahsula 'alaa al-maziid mina al-khubz, min fadlik* هل يمكن ان احصل على المزيد من الخبز من فضلك
Could I have another bottle of water/wine, please?	*Hal yumkin an ahsula 'alaa zujajat maa'/nabidh ukhraa min fadlik* هل يمكن أن أحصل على زجاجة ماء/نبيذ أخري من فضلك؟
Could I have another portion of..., please?	*Hal yumkin an ahsula 'alaa qit'a ukhraa min..., min fadlik* هل يمكن ان احصل على قطعة اخرى من ...من فضلك
Could I have the salt and pepper, please?	*Hal yumkin an ahsula 'alaa milh wa fulful, min fadlik* هل يمكن ان احصل على ملح وفلفل من فضلك

Could I have a napkin, please?

Hal yumkin an ahsula 'alaa mindiil, min fadlik

هل يمكن ان احصل على منديل من فضلك

Could I have a teaspoon, please?

Hal yumkin an ahsula 'alaa mil'aqa, min fadlik

هل يمكن ان احصل على ملعقة من فضلك

Could I have an ashtray, please?

Hal yumkin an ahsula 'alaa..., min fadlik

هل يمكن ان احصل على...من فضلك

Could I have some matches, please?

Hal yumkin an ahsula 'alaa kibriit, min fadlik

هل يمكن ان احصل على كبريت من فضلك

Could I have some toothpicks, please?

Hal yumkin an ahsul 'alaa a'waad tanziif al-asnaan, min fadlik

هل يمكن ان احصل على اعواد تنظيف الاسنان من فضلك

Could I have a glass of water, please?

Hal yumkin an ahsulu 'alaa ka's maa', min fadlik

هل يمكن ان احصل على كأس ماء من فضلك

Could I have a straw, please?

Hal yumkin an ahsula 'alaa siifuna (massaasa lish-shuurb), min fadlik

هل يمكن ان احصل على سيفونة (مصاصة للشرب) من فضلك

Enjoy your meal!

Wajba shahiyya!

وجبة شهية

You too!

Wa anta kadhaalik!

وانت كذلك

Cheers!

Sahtiin!

صحتين

The next round's on me

Al-marra al-qaadima 'alaa hisaabii anaa

المرة القادمة على حسابي أنا

| Could we have a doggy bag, please? | *Law samaht, hal yumkin an nahsula 'alaa kiis li-lkalb?* |
| | لو سمحت هل يمكن ان نحصل على كيس للكلب؟ |

4.3 The bill

See also 8.2 Settling the bill

How much is this dish?	*Bikam si'ru haadhaa t-tabaq?*
	بكم سعر هذا الطبق؟
Could I have the bill, please?	*Al-faatuura min fadlik?*
	الفاتورة من فضلك؟
All together	*Jamii'an*
	جميعا
Everyone pays separately	*Kul waahid yadfa' 'an nafsihi*
	كل واحد يدفع عن نفسه
Could we have the menu again, please?	*Hal yumkin an nahsala 'alaa al-qaa'ima marratan ukhraa, min fadlik?*
	هل يمكن ان نحصل على القائمة مرة اخرى، من فضلك؟
The...is not on the bill	*Al...laysa fii l-faatuura*
	ال ...ليس في الفاتورة

4.4 Complaints

It's taking a very long time	*Laqad ta'akhara kathiiran*
	لقد تأخر كثيرا
We've been here an hour already	*Nahnu hunaa mundhu sa'aa*
	نحن هنا منذ ساعة
This must be a mistake	*Haadhaa khata' bit-ta'kiid*
	هذا خطأ بالتأكيد

This is not what I ordered	*Laysa haadhaa maa talabtu* ليس هذا ما طلبت
I ordered...	*Anaa talabtu...* انا طلبت...
There's a dish missing	*Hunnaka tabaq mafquud* هناك طبق مفقود
This is broken/not clean	*Haadhaa maksuur/wasikh* هذا مكسور/وسخ
The food's cold	*At-ta'aamu baarid* الطعام بارد
The food's not fresh	*At-ta'aamu laysa tazajan* الطعام ليس طازجا
The food's too salty/ sweet/spicy	*At-ta'aamu maalih/huluw/haar jiddan* الطعام ملح/حلو/حار جدا
The meat's too rare	*Al-lahmu laysa mathuw jayyidan* اللحم ليس مطهو جيدا
The meat's overdone	*Al-lahmu matbuukh akthar min al-laazim* اللحم مطبوخ اكثر من اللازم
The meat's tough	*Al-lahmu laysa tariyyan* اللحم ليس طريا
The meat is off/ has gone bad	*Al-lahmu faasid/radii'* اللحم فاسد/رديء
Could I have something else instead of this?	*Hal yumkin an ahsula 'alaa shay' ghayr haadhaa?* هل يمكن أن أحصل على شيء غير هذا؟
The bill/this amount is not right	*Al-faatuura/haadhaa al-mablagh laysa sahiihan* الفاتورة/هذا المبلغ ليس صحيحا
We didn't have this	*Lam na'kul haadhaa* لم نأكل هذا

There's no toilet paper in the restroom	*Laa yuujad waraq kliiniks (awraaq twaaliit) fii al-maraafiq as-sihhiyya* لا يوجد ورق كلينكس (اوراق تواليت) في المرافق الصحية
Will you call the manager, please?	*Hal laka an tunaadi al-mudiir min fadlik?* هل لك أن تنادي المدير من فضلك

4.5 Paying a compliment

That was a wonderful meal	*Kaanat wajba raa'i'a* كانت وجبة رائعة
The food was excellent	*Kaana at-ta'aamu mumtaazan* كان الطعام ممتازا
The...in particular was delicious	*Bil-khussuus kaana al-... ladhiidhan* بالخصوص كان ال...لذيذا

4.6 The menu

مقبلات *muqabbilaat* starter/hors d'oeuvres	لعبة *lu'ba* game	لحم *lahm* meat	أجرة *ujra* cover charge
طبق غير اساسي/ خضروات *tabaq ghayr assaasi/ khudrawaat* side dishes/vegetables	جبن *jubn (jibn)* cheese	سمك *samak* fish	المفتحات *al-mufattihaat* first course
آداء القيمة المضافة *adaa' al-qiima al-mudaafa* VAT	فواكه *fawaakih* fruit	بيزا *piizaa* pizza	أجرة الخدمة *ujrat al-khidma* service charge
	بوظة *buuza* ice cream	شوربة *shurba* soup	طبق خاص *tabak khaas* specialities

شراب	خضروات	خبز	وجبات خفيفة
sharaab	**khudrawaat**	**khubz**	**wajabaat khafiifa**
liqueur (after dinner)	vegetables	bread	snacks
الوجبة الرئيسية	معكرونة	سلطة	كعك/حلويات
al-wajba ar-ra'isiyya	**ma'karuuna**	**salata**	**ka'k/halawiyyaat**
main course	pasta	salad	cakes/desserts

4.7 Alphabetical list of drinks and dishes

juice	*'asiir* عصير
rice	*aruz* أرز
orange	*burtuqaal* برتقال
chicken	*dajaaj* دجاج
strawberry	*faraawla* فراولة
fruit	*fawaakih* فواكه
pepper	*fulful* فلفل
spicy/hot	*haar* حار
sweets/cakes	*halawiyyaat* حلويات
cheese	*jubn* جبن
cakes	*k'ak* كعك
bread	*khubz* خبز
vegetables	*khudrawaat* خضروات
meat	*lahm* لحم
pasta	*ma'karuuna* معكرونة
water	*maa'* ماء
banana	*mawz* موز
pickled vegetables	*mikhallil* مخلل

salt	milh ملح
first course	muqabbilaat مقبلات
pizza	piizaa بيزا
coffee	qahwa قهوة
fish	samak سمك
tea	shaay شاي
apples	tuffaah تفاح
main dish	wajba ra'isiyya وجبة رئيسية
olives	zaytuun زيتون

Eating out

4

4.8 Well-known dishes

ملوخية
mulukhiyah
corchorus (green leafy vegetable
  of the mallow family)

فلافل
falafel
fried balls made from ground
  chickpeas or fava beans

مندي
mandii
basmati rice dish containing
  spices and tandoor-cooked meat

تبولة
tabbouleh
salad of cracked wheat

كبسة
kabsah
rice dish containing spices,
  meat and vegetables

كباب
kabab
kebab

بقلاوة
baqlawah
baklava

5 Getting Around

5. Getting Around

5.1 Asking directions

Excuse me, could I ask you something?	*Law samahta, hal yumkin an as'alaka su'aalan?* لو سمحت هل يمكن أن أسألك سؤالا؟
I've lost my way	*Laqad dalltu tariiqii* لقد ضللت طريقي
Is there a...around here?	*Hal yuujad...hunaa?* هل يوجد...هنا؟
Is this the way to...?	*Hal haadhaa huwa at-tariiqu ilaa..?* هل هذا هو الطريق إلى...؟
Could you tell me how to get to...?	*Hal tadullanii 'alaa...?* هل تدلني على...؟
What's the quickest way to...?	*Maa huwa asra' tariiq ilaa...?* ما هو أسرع طريق إلى...؟
How many kilometers is it to...?	*Kam killumitr (al-massafa) ilaa...?* كم كيلو متر (المسافة) إلى...؟
Could you point it out on the map?	*Hal tubayyin lii dhaalika 'alaa alkhaarita?* هل تبين لي ذلك على الخارطة؟

لا أعرف، لا أعرف طريقي هنا	I don't know, I don't know my way around here
أنت ذاهب في الطريق الخطأ	You're going the wrong way
يجب أن ترجع إلى...	You have to go back to...

بعد ذلك اتبع العلامات		From there on just follow the signs
عندما تصل إلى هناك اسأل مرة أخرى		When you get there, ask again

النفق	الطريق/الشارع	سر إلى الأمام
an-nafaq	*at-tariiq/ash-shaari'*	*sir 'ila l-'amaam*
the tunnel	the road/street	go straight ahead
اعبر	المعبر	انعطف يسارا
u'bur	*al-ma'bar*	*in'atif yas'aran*
cross	the overpass	turn left
اتبع	علامة الخروج	انعطف يمينا
ittabi'	*'alaamat al-khuruuj*	*in'atif yamiinan*
follow	the "yield" sign	turn right
النهر	البناية	الإشارة الضوئية
an-nahr	*al-binaaya*	*al-ishaara ad-daw'iyya*
the river	the building	the traffic light
الجسر	عند الزاوية	التقاطع
al-jisr	*'inda z-zaawiya*	*at-taqaat'u*
the bridge	at the corner	the intersection/crossroads
السهم	ممر العبور	العلامات تشير إلى
as-sahm	*mamarr al-'ubuur*	*al-al'aamaat tushiir ilaa*
the arrow	the grade crossing	the signs pointing to

5.2 Traffic signs

أولوية المرور	أنر المصابيح الامامية في النفق
awlawiyyat al-muruur	*anir al-masabiih al-amaamiya fii al-nafaq*
right of way	turn on headlights (in the tunnel)

قف
qif
stop

محطة بنزين
mahattat banziin
service station

إحذر
ihdhar
beware

شاحنات ثقيلة
shaahinaat thaqiila
heavy truck

ممر مغلق
mamarr mughlaq
impassable shoulder

أشغال على الطريق
ashghaal 'alaa t-tariiq
road works

تغيير مسارات
taghyiir masaaraat
change lanes

رواق طوارىء
riwaaq haarat
emergency lane

منعطفات
mun'atafaat
curves

تغيير وجهة
taghyiir wijha
detour

ممنوع الدخول
mamnuu' ad-dukhuul
no entry

أولوية المرور عند نهاية الطريق
awlawiyyat al-muruur 'inda nihaayat at-tariiq
right of way at end of road

تقاطع
taqqaatu'
intersection/crossroads

لا تعرقل سير الطريق
laa tu'arqil sayra t-tariiq
do not obstruct

إحذر، صخور متساقطة
ihdhar, sukhuur mutasaaqita
beware, falling rocks

أجرة رسوم الطريق
ujrat rusuum at-tariiq
toll payment

موقف سيارات بأجرة/موقف محجوز
mawqif sayyaaraat bi'ujra/mawqif mahjuuz
paying carpark/parking reserved for

موقف سيارات مراقب
mawqif sayyaaraat muraaqab
supervised parking

موقف إجباري
mawqif ijbaarii
parking disk (compulsory)

ممر مقطوع/ممر مسدود امام للمترجلين
mamarr maqtuu'/mamarr masduud amaama al-mutarajjiliin
no access/no pedestrian access

ستسحب السيارات في هذه المنطقة
sa-tushab as-sayyaaraat fii haadhihi l-mintaqa
tow-away area (both sides of the road)

ممر للعبور...
mamarr li-l'ubuur
grade crossing

العدد الأقصى للركاب
al-'ada al-aqsaa lir-rukkaab
maximum headroom

ممنوع المرور
mamnuu' al-muruur
no passing

جزيرة مرور/طريق للمترجلين
tariiq lil-mutarajjiliin/jazira muruur
traffic island/pedestrian walk

خطر
khatar
danger(ous)

طريق متعرج
tariiq muta'arrij
broken/uneven surface

مدخل
madkhal
driveway

إبق على اليسار/اليمين
ibqa 'alaa al-yasaar/al-yamiin
keep right/left

الطريق مقفل
at-tariiq muqfal
road blocked

مطر أو ثلج بعد...كيلومتر
matar aw thalj ba'da... kiilumitr
rain or ice for...kms

نفق
nafaq
tunnel

السرعة القصوى
as-sur'a al-quswaa
maximum speed

خفف السرعة
khaffif as-sur'a
slow down

موقف مؤقت
mawqif mu'aqqat
parking for a limited period

إتجاه واحد
ittijaah waahid
one way

ممنوع إيقاف السيارات
mamnuu' 'iiqaf as-sayyaaraat
no hitchhiking

خروج
khuruuj
exit

ممنوع الإانعطف يمينا أو يسارا
mamnuu' al-in'itaaf yamiinan aw yasaaran
no right or left turn

الطريق مغلق
at-tariiq mughlaq
road closed

مساعدة على الطريق
musaa'ada 'alaa t-tariiq
road assistance (breakdown service)

دائرة قرصية
daa'ira qursiyya
disk zone

طريق ضيق
tariiq dayyiq
narrowing in the road

5.3 The car

See the diagram on page 81

● **Speed limits**

On freeways 110 km/h for cars; on all main, non-urban highways 100 km/h; on secondary, non-urban highways 80 km/h; in
built-up areas 50 km/h.

Give way to vehicles coming from the right unless otherwise
indicated. Towing prohibited to private drivers.

5.4 The gas station

● The cost of gas in the Middle East varies from one country to
another but surprisingly high (around $1 per 1 liter), slightly
less for unleaded.

How many kilometers to the next gas station, please?	*Law samahta kam kiilumitr tab'ud mahattat al-banziin al-qaadima?* لو سمحت كم كيلومترا تبعد محطة البنزين القادمة؟
I'd like...liters of...	*Uriidu...litran min...* أريد...ليترا من
– super	*rafii'* رفيع
– leaded	*makhluut* مخلوط
– unleaded	*biduun rasaas* بدون رصاص
– diesel	*diizil* ديزل
...dollars worth of gas	*...maa qiimatuhu min l-banziin* ...ما قيمته من البنزين

The parts of a car

(the diagram shows the numbered parts)

1	battery	بطارية	*battariyya*
2	rear light	الضوء الخلفي	*ad-daw'u al-khalfiy*
3	rear-view mirror	المرآة الخلفية	*al-mir'aat al-khalfiyya*
	backup light	الضوء الإحتياطي	*ad-daw'u al-ihtiyaatiy*
4	aerial	الهوائي	*al-hawaa'ii*
	car radio	راديو السيارة	*radyu as-sayyara*
5	gas tank	خزان الوقود	*khazzan al-waquud*
6	spark plugs	شمعات القدح	*shama'aat al-qadh*
	fuel pump	مضخة الوقود	*madakhat al-waquud*
7	side mirror	المرآة الجانبية	*al-mir'aat al-jaanibiyya*
8	bumper	مخفف الصدمة	*mukhaffif as-sadma*
	carburettor	جهاز مزج الوقود (كبريتر)	*jihaaz mazj al-waquud (kabraytar)*
	crankcase	علبة التدوير	*'ulbat at-tadwiir*
	cylinder	أسطوانة	*istuwaana*
	ignition	قدح	*qadh*
	warning light	ضوء تحذير	*daw' tahdhiir*
	generator	مولد	*muwallid*
	accelerator	دواسة السرعة	*dawwaasat as-sur'a*
	handbrake	الفرامل اليدوية	*al-faraamil al-yadawiyya*
	valve	صمام	*sammam*
9	muffler	كمامة	*kamaama*
10	trunk	صندوق السيارة	*sunduuq as-sayyaara*
11	headlight	الضوء الأمامي	*ad-daw'u al-amaami*
	crank shaft	عمود المحرك	*'amuud al-muharrik*
12	air filter	مصفاة الهواء	*misfaat al-hawaa'*
	fog lamp	مصباح ضباب	*misbaah dabaab*
13	engine block	كتلة المحرك	*kutlat al-muhrrik*
	camshaft	عمود الحدبات	*'amuud al-hadabaat*
	oil filter/pump	مصفاة زيت	*misfaat zayt*
	dipstick	الخطرة/مقياس الزيت	*al-khatra/miqyas az-sayt*
	pedal	دواسة	*dawwasa*
14	door	باب	*baab*
15	radiator	راديتر	*radaytar*
16	brake disc	قرص الفرامل	*qurs al-faraamil*
	spare wheel	عجلة احتياطية	*'ajalat ihtiyaatiyya*
17	indicator	مؤشر	*mu'ashir*
18	windshield wiper	ماسحة	*maasiha*
19	shock absorbers	واقيات التعثر	*waaqiyat at-ta'athur*
	sunroof	سقف السيارة	*saqf as-sayyaara*
	spoiler	اللوحة الخلفية للسيارة	*al-lawhat al-khalfiya lis-sayyaara*
20	steering column	عمود المقود	*'amuud al-miqwad*
	steering wheel	المقود	*al-miqwad*

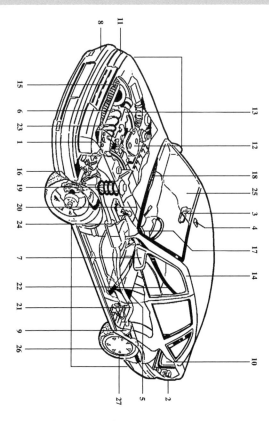

21	exhaust pipe	أنبوب الدخان	*unbuub ad-dukhaan*
22	seat belt	حزام الأمان	*hizaam al-'amaan*
	fan	مروحة	*mirwaha*
23	distributor cables	موزع أسلاك	*muwazzi' aslaak*
24	gear shift	محول السرعة	*muhawwil as-sur'a*
25	windshield	الزجاج الأمامي	*az-zujaaj al-amaami*
	water pump	مضخة الماء	*midakhat al-maa'*
26	wheel	العجلة	*al-'ajala*
27	hubcap	غطاء واقي	*ghitaa' waqii*
	piston	مكبس	*mikbas*

Manual or automatic?	يدوية أم أوتوماتيكية؟	*Yadawiya am automaticiya?*
Global Positioning System (GPS)	نظام تحديد الموقع العالمي (جي بي إس)	*Nizaam tahdiid al-mawaqi' al-'alamii (GPS)*

Fill it up, please	*Imlaaha hunaa min fadlik* املأها من فضلك
Could you check...?	*Hal yumkin an tafhasa...?* هل يمكن أن تفحص...؟
– the oil level	*mustawaa az-zayt* مستوى الزيت
– the tire pressure	*daght al-hawaa' fii l-'ajalaat* ضغط الهواء في العجلات
Could you change the oil, please?	*Hal yumkin an tughayyira az-zayt min fadlik?* هل يمكن أن تغير الزيت من فضلك؟
Could you clean the windshield, please?	*Hal tunazzif az-zujaaj al-amaami min fadlik?* هل تنظف الزجاج الأمامي من فضلك؟
Could you wash the car, please?	*Hal taghsil lii as-sayyaara min fadlik?* هل تغسل لي السيارة من فضلك؟

5.5 Breakdowns and repairs

I have broken down, could you give me a hand?	*Taattalat sayyaaratii, mumkin tusaa'idunii min fadlik?* تعطلت سيارتي ممكن تساعدني من فضلك؟
I've run out of gas	*Laysa ladayya banziin/nafadha ladayya al-banziin* ليس لدي بنزين/نفذ لدي البنزين
I've locked the keys in the car	*Aqfaltu as-sayyaara wa fiihaa almiftaah* اقفلت السيارة وفيها المفاتيح
The car/motorbike/ moped won't start	*Sayyaaratii/darraajatii/laa tashtaghil (laa ta'mal)* سيارتي/دراجتي/لا تشتغل (لا تعمل)

Could you contact the breakdown service for me, please?	*Hal yumkin an tattasila bikhidmat as-siyaana min fadlik?* هل يمكن ان تتصل بخدمة الصيانة من فضلك؟
Could you call a garage for me, please?	*Hal yumkin an tattasil biwarshat tasliih min fadlik?* هل يمكن ان تتصل بورشة تصليح من فضلك؟
Could you give me a lift to...?	*Hal yumkin an tuusilanii bisayyaaratik illa...min fadlik?* هل يمكن أن توصلني بسيارتك إلى... من فضلك؟
– the nearest garage?	*ilaa aqrab warshat tasliih?* إلى اقرب ورشة تصليح؟
– the nearest town?	*ilaa aqrab madiina?* إلى اقرب مدينة؟
– the nearest telephone booth?	*ilaa aqrab haatif 'umuumii?* إلى اقرب هاتف عمومي؟
– the nearest emergency phone?	*ilaa aqrab haatif tawaari'?* إلى اقرب هاتف طواريء؟
Can we take my moped?	*Hal yumkin an na'khudha darraajatii?* هل يمكن ان نأخذ دراجتي؟
Could you tow me to a garage?	*Hal yumkin an tashaba sayyaaratii ilaa aqrab warshat tasliih?* هل يمكن ان تسحب سيارتي إلى اقرب ورشة تصليح؟
There's probably something wrong with the... (See 5.3)	*Rubbamaa takuun hunaaka mushkila fii al-...* ربما تكون هناك مشكلة في الـ...
Can you fix it?	*Hal tastatii an tuslihaha?* هل تستطيع ان تصلحها؟
Could you fix my tire?	*Hal yumkin an tusliha ajaltii (duulabii)?* هل يمكنك ان تصلح عجلتي/دولابي؟

Could you change this wheel?	*Hal yumkin an tughayyira haadha d-duulaab?*
	هل يمكن ان تغير هذا الدولاب؟
Can you fix it so it'll get me to...?	*Hal yumkin islaahuhu bihaythu yuusilunii ilaa...?*
	هل يمكن اصلاحه بحيث يوصلني إلى...؟
Which garage can help me?	*Ayyatu warshat tasliih yumkin an tusaa'idanii?*
	اية ورشة تصليح يمكن ان تساعدني؟
When will my car/bicycle be ready?	*Mata satakuun sayyaaratii/darraajatii jaahiza?*
	متى ستكون سيارتي/دراجتي جاهزة؟
Have you already finished?	*Hal intahayta?*
	هل انتهيت؟
Can I wait for it here?	*Hal yumkin an antazira hunaa?*
	هل يمكن ان انتظر هنا؟
How much will it cost?	*kam sayukallif islaahuhaa?*
	كم سيكلف اصلاحها؟
Could you itemize the bill?	*Hal yumkin an taktuba al-faatuura bit-tafsiil?*
	هل يمكن أن تكتب الفاتورة بالتفصيل؟
Could you give me a receipt for insurance purposes?	*Hal yumkin an tu'tiyanii waslan bi-dhaalik?*
	هل يمكن ان تعطيني وصلا بذلك؟

5.6 Bicycles/mopeds

See the diagram on page 87

Bicycle paths are rare in the Middle East and, therefore, not much consideration for bikes should be expected on the roads. The maximum speed for mopeds is 40 km/h but you should be aged 14 and over. A crash helmet is compulsory up to the age of

18, and a new law is being considered to make helmets compulsory for anyone. This should be checked when you arrive.

لا توجد لدي قطع غيار لسيارتك/دراجتك	I don't have parts for your car/bicycle
يجب ان اجلب القطع من مكان اخر	I have to get the parts from somewhere else
يجب أن اطلب القطع	I have to order the parts
هذا يحتاج إلى نصف يوم	That'll take half a day
هذا يحتاج إلى يوم كامل	That'll take a day
هذا يحتاج إلى بضعة أيام	That'll take a few days
هذا يحتاج إلى أسبوع	That'll take a week
سيارتك ستعوضها شركة التأمين	Your car is a write-off
لا يمكن إصلاحها	It can't be repaired
السيارة/الدراجة النارية/الدراجة الآلية/الدراجة ستكون حاضرة الساعة...	The car/motor bike/moped/bicycle will be ready at...o'clock

5.7 Renting a vehicle

I'd like to rent a...	*Uriidu an asta'jira...* أريد ان استأجر...
Do I need a (special) license for that?	*Hal ahtaaju ilaa rukhsat qiyaada khaassa li-dhaalik?* هل احتاج إلى رخصة قيادة خاصة لذلك؟
I'd like to rent the...for...	*Uriidu an asta'jir al-...li-muddat ...* أريد ان استأجر ال...لمدة...
– the...for a day	*Al-...li-yawmin waahid* ال...ليوم واحد

The parts of a bicycle

(The diagram shows the numbered parts)

1	rear light	الإضاءة الخلفية	*al-idaa'a l-khalfiyya*
2	rear wheel	العجلة الخلفية	*al-'ajala al-khalfiyya*
3	(luggage) carrier	حمال	*hammal*
4	fork	عمود	*'amuud*
5	bell	جرس	*jaras*
6	pedal crank	ذراع الدواسة	*dhiraa ad-dawwaasa*
7	gear change wire	تغيير السرعة	*taghyiir as-sur'a*
		سلك	*silk*
	generator	مولد	*muwwallid*
	bicycle trailer	عربة مجرورة بدراجة	*'araba majruura bi-darraja*
	frame	إطار	*itaar*
8	wheel guard	واقية العجلة	*waaqiyat al-'ajala*
9	chain	سلسلة	*silsila*
	chain guard	واقي السلسة	*waaqii as-silsila*
	odometer	عداد المسافة	*'addad al-masaafa*
	child's seat	مقعد أطفال	*maq'ad atfaal*
10	headlight	الاضاءة الامامية	*al-idaa'a al-amaamiyya*
	bulb	مصباح	*misbaah*
11	pedal	دواسة	*dawwaasa*
12	pump	مضخة	*midakha*
13	reflector	العاكس	*al-'aakis*
14	brake shoe	دواسة الفرامل	*dawwaasat al-faraamil*
15	brake cable	سلك الفرامل	*silk al-faraamil*
16	anti-theft device	منبه ضد السرقة	*munabbih did as-sariqa*
17	carrier straps	الأحزمة الناقلة	*al-ahzima an-naaqila*
	tachometer	مقياس سرعة الدوران	*miqyaas sur'at ad-dawaraan*
18	spoke	شعاع الدولاب	*shu'aa' ad-duulaab*
19	mudguard	واقية	*waaqiya*
20	handlebar	مقود الراجة	*miqwad ad-darraja*
21	chain wheel	السلسة الدولابية	*as-silsila ad-dulaabiya*
	toe clip	مشبك الجر	*mishbak al-jarr*
22	crank axle	محور التدوير	*mihwar at-tadwiir*
	drum brake	إسطوانة الفرامل	*istiwaanat al-faraamil*
23	rim	حافة	*haaffat*
24	valve	صمام	*sammaam*

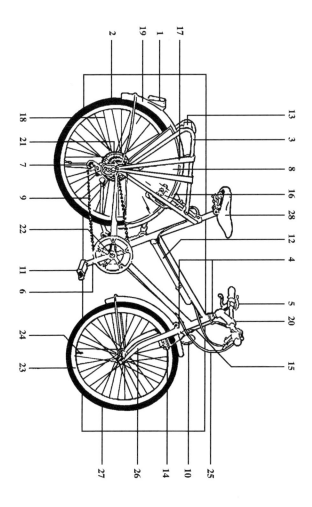

25	gear cable	سلك مغير السرعة	*silk mughayir as-sur'a*
26	fork	عمود	*'amuud*
27	front wheel	العجلة الامامية	*al-'ajala al-amaamiyya*
28	seat	مقعد	*maq'ad*

– the...for two days	*Al-...li-yawmayn* ال...ليومين
How much is that per day/week?	*Kam al-ujra lil-yawm al-waahid/lil-'usbuu'?* كم الاجرة لليوم الواحد/الاسبوع؟
How much is the deposit?	*Kam yajibu an adfa'a muqaddaman?* كم يجب أن ادفع مقدما؟
Could I have a receipt for the deposit?	*Hal yumkin an tu'tiyanii waslan bil-mablagh al-madfuu'?* هل يمكن أن تعطيني وصلا بالمبلغ المدفوع؟
How much is the surcharge per kilometer?	*Kam al-ujra al-idaafiyya likul kiilumitr?* كم الاجرة الاضافية لكل كيلومتر؟
Does that include gas?	*Hal haadhaa yashmal al-banziin?* هل هذا يشمل البنزين؟
Does that include insurance?	*Hal haadhaa yashmal rusuum at-ta'miin?* هل هذا يشمل رسوم التأمين؟
What time can I pick the ...up?	*Mataa yumkin an aakhudha al-...?* متى يمكن أن آخذ ال...؟
When does it have to be back?	*Mataa yajib an u'iida?* متى يجب أن أعيد؟
Where's the gas tank?	*Ayna khazzan al-banziin?* أين خزان البنزين؟
What sort of fuel does it take?	*Maa naw'u banziin sayyaratik?* ما نوع بنزين سيارتك؟

5.8 Hitchhiking

Where are you heading?	*Ilaa ayna anta dhaahib?* إلى أين انت ذاهب؟

Can you give me a lift?	*Hal yumkin an tuusilanii bi-sayyaritik?*
	هل يمكن أن توصلني بسيارتك؟
Can my friend (f) come too?	*Hal tastatii'u sadiiqatii an ta'tiya ma'ii?*
	هل تستطيع صديقتي أن تأتي معي؟
Can my friend (m) come too?	*Hal yastatii'u sadiiqii an ya'tiya ma'ii?*
	هل يستطيع صديقي أن يأتي معي؟
I'd like to go to...	*Uriidu an adhhaba ilaa...*
	أريد أن أذهب إلى...
Is that on the way to...?	*Hal haadhaa huwa at-tariiq ilaa...?*
	هل هذا هو الطريق إلى...؟
Could you drop me off?	*Hal yumkin an tunzilanii 'inda?*
	هل يمكن أن تنزلني عند؟
Could you drop me off here?	*Hal yumkin an tunzilanii hunaa?*
	هل يمكن أن تنزلني هذا؟
– at the entrance to the highway?	*'inda madkhal at-tariiq as-sayyaara?*
	عند مدخل الطريق السيارة؟
– in the center?	*wasat al-madiina?*
	وسط المدينة؟
- at the next intersection?	*'inda at-taqaat'u al-qaadim?*
	عند التقاطع القادم؟
Could you stop here, please?	*Hal yumkin an tatawaqqafa hunaa min fadlik?*
	هل يمكن أن تتوقف هنا من فضلك؟
I'd like to get out here	*Uriidu an anzila hunaa*
	أريد أن أنزل هنا
Thanks for the lift	*Shukran 'alaa al-musaa'ada*
	شكرا على المساعدة

6 Arrival and Departure

6. Arrival and Departure

6.1 General

● Bus tickets are purchased at bus stations or on board the bus, and must be shown to the conductor when required. Single tickets can be bought in blocks of four.

قطار الساعة...المتوجه إلى...تأخر...دقائق	The [time] train to...has been delayed by... minutes
القطار المتوجه إلى...يصل الان إلى الرصيف...	The train to...is now arriving at platform...
القطار القادم من...يصل الان الى الرصيف...	The train from...is now arriving at platform...
القطار المتوجه إلى...سيغادر من الرصيف...	The train to...will leave from platform...
قطار الساعة...المتوجه إلى...سوف يغادر اليوم من الرصيف...	Today the [time] train to... will leave from platform...
المحطة القادمة هي...	The next station is...

Where does this train go to?
Ilaa ayna yadhhab haadha l-qitaar?
إلى أين يذهب هذا القطار؟

Does this boat go to...?
Hal haadha al-markab dhaahib ilaa...?
هل هذا المركب ذاهب إلى...؟

Can I take this bus to...?
Hal astatii' an arkaba haadha al-baas ilaa...?
هل استطيع ان اركب هذا الباص إلى...؟

Does this train stop at...?
Hal yatawaqqaf haadha al-qitaar 'inda...?
هل يتوقف هذا القطار عند...؟

Is this seat taken/free?	*Hal haadha al-maq'ad mahjuuz/ faarigh?*
	هل هذا المقعد محجوز/فارغ؟
I've reserved...	*Anaa ladyya hajz...*
	انا لدي حجز...
Could you tell me where I have to get off for...?	*Hal tastatii' an tukhbiranii ayna yajibu an anzila ilaa...?*
	هل تستطيع ان تخبرني اين يجب ان انزل إلى...؟
Could you let me know when we get to...?	*Hal yumkin an tukhbiranii 'indamaa nasil ilaa...?*
	هل يمكن ان تخبرني عندما نصل إلى...؟
Could you stop at the next stop, please?	*Hal yumkin an tatawaqqaf 'inda al-mawqif al-qaadim, min fadlik?*
	هل يمكن ان تتوقف عند الموقف القادم، من فضلك؟
Where are we?	*Ayna nahnu al-aan?*
	أين نحن الآن؟
Do I have to get off here?	*Hal yajibu an anzila hunaa?*
	هل يجب ان انزل هنا؟
Have we already passed...?	*Hal tajaawaznaa/'abarnaa...?*
	هل تجاوزنا/عبرنا...؟
Can I come back on the same ticket?	*Hal yumkin an a'uuda binafs at-tadhkira?*
	هل يمكن ان اعود بنفس التذكرة؟
Can I change on this ticket?	*Hal yumkin an ughayyira haadhihi at-tadhkira?*
	هل يمكن ان أغير هذه التذكرة؟
How long is this ticket valid for?	*Maa muddat salaahiyyat haadhihi t-tadhkira?*
	ما مدة صلاحية هذه التذكرة؟

How much is the extra fare for the high-speed train?	*Maa l-ujra al-idaafiyya lil-qitaar as-sarii'?* ما الاجرة الاضافية للقطار السريع؟

6.2 Customs

By law you must always carry with you a passport, and if driving, your driving license.

Most visitors require a visa to enter certain countries of the Middle East, and these should be organized prior to travel arrangements as procedures differ from one country to another.

For car and motorbike: valid driving license, vehicle registration document; third-party international insurance document.

Trailer: same registration number plate and registration documents.

جواز السفر من فضلك	Your passport, please
البطاقة الخضراء من فضلك	Your green card, please
وثائق سيارتك من فضلك	Your vehicle documents, please
التأشيرة من فضلك	Your visa, please
إلى أين أنت ذاهب؟	Where are you going?
كم يوما ستبقى هنا؟	How long are you planning to stay?
هل لديك ما تصرح به؟	Do you have anything to declare?
إفتح هذا من فضلك	Open this, please

Import and export specifications:
Foreign currency – no restrictions
Alcohol   – prohibited in some countries (Saudi Arabia), but allowed under strict regulations in others (Syria)

Tobacco   – 200 cigarettes, 50 cigars, 250g tobacco
Perfume – 50g perfume, 250ml eau de toilette
Coffee   – 500g
Tea   – 100g

My children are entered on this passport	*Atfaalii musajjaluun fii haadha l-jawaaz*
	أطفالي مسجلون في هذا الجواز
I'm traveling through	*Anaa musaafir 'an tariiq*
	أنا مسافر عن طريق
I'm going on vacation to...	*Anaa dhaahib fii nuzha ilaa...*
	أنا ذاهب في نزهة إلى...
I'm on a business trip	*Anaa fii rihlat 'amal*
	أنا في رحلة عمل
I don't know how long I'll be staying	*Laa a'rif kam sa'abqaa*
	لا أعرف كم سأبقى
I'll be staying here for a weekend	*Sa-abqaa hunaa ilaa nihaayat al-usbuu*
	سأبقى هنا إلى نهاية الأسبوع
I'll be staying here for a few days	*Sa-uqiimu hunaa li-bid'at ayyaam*
	سأقيم هنا لبضعة أيام
I'll be staying here a week	*Sa-'abqaa hunaa usbuu'an*
	سأبقى هنا أسبوعا
I'll be staying here for two weeks	*Sa-'abqaa hunaa usbuu'ayn*
	سأبقى هنا أسبوعين
I've got nothing to declare	*Laysa ladayya shay' usariih bihi*
	ليس لدي شيء أصرح به
I have...	*Ladayya...*
	لدي...
– a carton of cigarettes	*kartuunat sajaa'ir*
	كرتونة سجائر
– a bottle of...	*zujajat...*
	زجاجة...

– some souvenirs

ba'd al-hadaayaa
بعض الهدايا

These are personal items

Haadhihi amti'a shakhsiya
هذه أمتعة شخصية

These are not new

Haadhihi laysat jadiida
هذه ليست جديدة

Here's the receipt

Haadhaa huwa al-wasl
هذا هو الوصل

This is for private use

Haadhaa lil-istikhdaam al-khaas
هذا للإستخدام الخاص

How much import duty
do I have to pay?

*Kam yajibu an adfa'a rusuum
jumrukiyya?*
كم يجب أن أدفع رسوم جمركية؟

May I go now?

Hal astatii'u an adhhaba al'aan?
هل أستطيع أن أذهب الآن؟

6.3 Luggage

Porter!

Hammaal
حمال

Could you take this
luggage to...?

*Hal tastatii'u an tahmila haadhihi
al-badaa'i' ilaa ...?*
هل تستطيع أن تحمل هذه البضائع إلى...؟

How much do I owe you?

Kam adfa' laka?
كم أدفع لك؟

Where can I find a cart?

Ayna yumkin an ajida 'araba?
أين يمكن أن أجد عربة؟

Could you store this
luggage for me?

*Hal yumkin an takhzina lii haadhihi
al-badaa'i'?*
هل يمكن أن تخزن لي هذه البضائع؟

Where are the luggage lockers?	*Ayna <u>kh</u>izaanat hif<u>z</u> al-ba<u>d</u>aa'i'?* أين خزانة حفظ البضائع؟
I can't get the locker open	*Hal asta<u>t</u>ii'u an afta<u>h</u>a al-<u>kh</u>izaana* هل أستطيع أن أفتح الخزانة
How much is it per item per day?	*Kam yajib an adfa'a fii al-yawm muqaabil kulli qi<u>t</u>'a?* كم يجب أن أدفع في اليوم مقابل كل قطعة؟
This is not my suitcase	*Haa<u>dh</u>ihi laysat <u>h</u>aqiibatii* هذه ليست حقيبتي
There's one item/suitcase missing	*Hunaaka <u>h</u>aqiiba/kiis mafquud* هناك حقيبة/كيس مفقود
My suitcase is damaged	*Haqiibatii taalifa* حقيبتي تالفة

6.4 Questions to passengers

Ticket types

درجة اولى ام ثانية؟	First or second class?
رحلة واحدة ام ذهاب واياب؟	Single or return?
للمدخنين ام غير المدخنين؟	Smoking or non-smoking?
مقعد بقرب الشباك؟	Window or aisle seat?
في مقدمة ام نهاية القطار؟	Front or back (of train)?
مقعد او سرير؟	Seat or berth?
الأعلى، في الوسط ام في الأسفل؟	Top, middle or bottom?
درجة سياحية او درجة اولى؟	Economy or first class?
حجرة او مقعد؟	Cabin or seat?
مفرد او مزدوج؟	Single or double?
كم عدد المسافرين؟	How many are traveling?

Destination

اين تريد السفر؟	Where are you travelling?
متى تريد السفر؟	When are you leaving?
...ك يغادر الساعة...	Your...leaves at...
عليك أن تغير	You have to change
عليك أن تنزل عند...	You have to get off at...
عليك أن تذهب عبر...	You have to go via...
رحلة الذهاب تكون...	The outward journey is on...
رحلة الاياب (العودة) تكون...	The return journey is on...
يجب أن تركب على الساعة...	You have to be on board by ...(o'clock)

Inside the vehicle

تذاكر السفر من فضلك	Tickets, please
الحجز من فضلك	Your reservation, please
جواز سفرك من فضلك	Your passport, please
انت في المقعد الخطأ	You're in the wrong seat
انت مخطئ/انت في ال...الخطأ	You have made a mistake/ You are in the wrong...
هذا المقعد محجوز	This seat is reserved
عليك ان تدفع اجرة اضافية	You'll have to pay extra
ال...تأخر...دقائق	The...has been delayed by... minutes

6.5 Tickets

Where can I...?	*Ayna yumkinunii an...?* اين يمكنني ان...؟
– buy a ticket	*ashtarii tadhkira* اشتري تذكرة
– reserve a seat	*ahjiz maq'ad* احجز مقعد
– book a flight	*ahjiz rihlat tayaraan* احجز رحلة طيران
Could I have...of..., please?	*Hal yumkin an ahsal 'alaa...li...min fadlik?* هل يمكن ان احصل على...ل. ...من فضلك؟
A single, please	*Tadhkirat rihla waahida min fadlik* تذكرة رحلة واحدة من فضلك
A return ticket, please	*Tadhkirat dhahaab wa iyaab min fadlik* تذكرة ذهاب وإياب من فضلك
– first class	*daraja uulaa* درجة اولى
– second class	*daraja thaaniya* درجة ثانية
– economy class	*daraja siyaahiya* درجة سياحية
I'd like to reserve a seat/ berth/cabin	*Uriidu an ahjiza maq'adan/sariiran/ hujratan* اريد ان احجز مقعدا/سريرا/حجرة

I'd like to reserve a top/
  middle/bottom berth in
  the sleeping car
	*Uriidu an ahjiza sariiran fii al-'alaa/
	al-wasat/al-asfal fii 'arabat an-nawm*
	اريد ان احجز سريرا في الاعلى/الوسط/
	الاسفل في عربة النوم

– by the window	*qurb a<u>sh</u>-<u>sh</u>ubbaak* قرب الشباك
– single/double	*mufrad/muzdawaj* مفرد /مزدوج
– at the front/back	*fii al-muqaddima/al-mu'a<u>kh</u>ara* في المقدمة/المؤخرة
There are...of us	*Na<u>h</u>nu...fardan* نحن...فردا
We have a car	*Ladaynaa sayyaara* لدينا سيارة
We have a trailer	*Ladaynaa 'araba sa<u>gh</u>iira* لدينا عربة صغيرة
We have...bicycles	*Ladaynaa...darrajaat hawa'iyya* لدينا...دراجات هوائية
Do you have a...?	*Hal ladayka...?* هل لديك...؟
– weekly travel card?	*tadhkirat safar usbuu'iyya?* تذكرة سفر اسبوعية؟
– monthly season ticket?	*tadhkirat safar <u>sh</u>ahriyya?* تذكرة سفر شهرية؟
Where's...?	*Ayna ...?* اين...؟
Where's the information desk?	*Ayna maktabu l-ma'luumaat?* اين مكتب المعلومات؟

6.6 Information

Where can I find a schedule?	*Ayna ajidu jadwalan bil-mawaa'iid?* اين اجد جدولا بالمواعيد؟

Where's the...desk?	*Ayna maktab al...?* اين مكتب ال...؟
Do you have a city map with the bus routes on it?	*Hal ladayka khaarita lilmadiina tahtawii 'alaa khutuut al-baasaat?* هل لديك خارطة للمدينة تحتوي على خطوط الباصات؟
Do you have a schedule?	*Hal ladayka qaa'ima bilmawaa'iid?* هل لديك قائمة بالمواعيد؟
Will I get my money back?	*Hal sa-'astarji'u nuquudii?* هل سأسترجع نقودي؟
I'd like to confirm/cancel/ change my reservation for trip to...	*Uriidu an u'akkida/ulghiya/ughayira l-hajz/ar-rihla ilaa...* اريد ان اؤكد/الغي/اغير الحجز/الرحلة الى...
I'd like to go to...	*Uriidu an adhhaba ilaa...* اريد ان اذهب الى...
What is the quickest way to get there?	*Maa huwa asra' tariiq lil-wusuul ilaa hunaak?* ماهو اسرع طريق للوصول الى هناك؟
How much is a single/ return to...?	*Maa si'r rihla waahida/rihla dhahaab wa iyaab ilaa ...?* كم سعر رحلة واحدة/رحلة ذهاب واياب الى...؟
Can I break my journey with this ticket?	*Hal yumkin an atawaqqafa fii makaanin maa bi-haadhihi at-tadhkira?* هل يمكن ان اتوقف في مكان ما بهذه التذكرة؟
Do I have to pay extra?	*Hal yajib an adfaa' ujuuran idaafiyya?* هل يجب ان ادفع اجورا اضافية؟
How much luggage am I allowed?	*Maa huwa al-had al-masmuuh bihi min al-amti'a/al-haqaa'ib?* ماهو الحد المسموح به من الامتعة/الحقائب؟

Is this a direct train?

Hal haadhaa qitaar mubaashir?

هل هذا قطار مباشر؟

Do I have to change?

Hal 'alayya an ughayyira?

هل علي ان اغير؟

Does the plane stop anywhere?

Hal tatawaqqaf at-taa'ira fii makaanin maa?

هل تتوقف الطائرة في مكان ما؟

Will there be any stop-overs?

Hal sayakun hunaaka ayya t-tawaqqufaat?

هل سيكون هناك اي توقفات؟

Does the boat stop at any other ports on the way?

Hal tatawaqqaf al-baakhira fii ba'd al-mawaani' khilaala r-rihla?

هل تتوقف الباخرة في بعض المواني خلال الرحلة؟

Does the train/bus stop at...?

Hal yatawaqqaf al-qitaar/al-baas 'inda...?

هل يتوقف القطار/الباص عند...؟

Where do I get off?

Ayna anzil?

اين انزل؟

Is there a connection to...?

Hal hunaaka takmila ilaa...?

هل هناك تكملة الى...؟

How long do I have to wait?

Maa hiya muddatu l-intizaar?

ما هي مدة الإنتظار؟

When does...leave?

Mataa yughaadir...?

متى يغادر...؟

What time does the first/next/last...leave?

Mataa yughaadir awwal/thaanii/aakhir...?

متى يغادر اول/ثاني/اخر...؟

How long does it take?

Kam tastaghriq ar-rihla?

كم تستغرق الرحلة؟

What time does...arrive in...?	*Mataa yasil al-...ilaa...?* متى يصل ال...الى...؟
Where does the...to... leave from?	*Min ayna yughaadir...al-muttawajjih ilaa...?* من اين يغادر...المتوجه الى...؟

6.7 Airports

On arrival at an Arabic airport (*mataar*), you will find the following signs:

تسليم الأمتعة *tasliim al-amti'a* check-in	دولي *duwalii* international	رحلات داخلية *rahalaat daakhiliyya* domestic flights
وصول *wusuul* arrivals	مغادرة *mughaadara* departures	

6.8 Trains

Train travel in the Middle East is simple and cheap. There are national railway companies in all countries of the region which offer services to the major cities. Services differ from one country to another, but overall you can expect a reasonable service frequency which does not always run on time. Tickets must be punched from the train station and shown at the entrance to platforms.

6.9 Taxis

There are plenty of taxis in all major cities with the cost varying substantially between very low in countries such as Syria and expensive in others such as the Gulf states. Taxis can be found in stands, especially at train and bus stations, or you can order taxis from your hotel reception with a surcharge sometimes payable for extra luggage and/or special pick up.

للاجرة li-l'ujra for hire	محجوز mahjuuz occupied	محطة سيارت الاجرة mahattat sayyaaraat al-ujra taxi stand

Taxi!	**Taaksi!** تاكسي
Could you get me a taxi, please?	**Hal yumkin an tatluba lii taaksi min fadlik?** هل يمكن ان تطلب لي تاكسي من فضلك؟
Where can I find a taxi around here?	**Ayna yumkin an ahsula 'alaa taaksi min hunaa?** اين يمكن ان احصل على تاكسي من هنا ؟
Could you take me to..., please?	**Hal yumkin an ta'khudhanii ilaa...min fadlik?** هل يمكن ان تاخذني الى...من فضلك؟
Could you take me to this address, please?	**Hal yumkin an ta'khudhanii ilaa haadhaa al-'unwaan min fadlik?** هل يمكن ان تاخذني الى هذا العنوان من فضلك؟
– to the...hotel, please	**ilaa funduq...min fadlik** الى فندق...من فضلك
– to the town/city center, please	**ilaa markadh al-madiina min fadlik** الى مركز المدينة من فضلك
– to the station, please	**ilaa l-mahatta min fadlik** الى المحطة من فضلك
– to the airport, please	**ilaa l-mataar min fadlik** الى المطار من فضلك

How much is the trip to...?	*Kam tukallif ar-rihla ilaa...?* كم تكلف الرحلة الى...؟
How far is it to...?	*Kam al-masaafa ilaa...?* كم المسافة الى...؟
Could you turn on the meter, please?	*Hal yumkin an tushaghila al-'addad min fadlik?* هل يمكن ان تشغل العداد من فضلك؟
I'm in a hurry	*Anaa 'alaa 'ajala* انا على عجلة
Could you speed up/ slow down a little?	*Hal yumkin an tusri'a/tukhaffifa mina s-sur'a?* هل يمكن ان تسرع/تخفف من السرعة
Could you take a different route?	*Hal yumkin an tasluka tariiqan aakhar?* هل يمكن ان تسلك طريقا اخر؟
I'd like to get out here, please	*Uriid an anzila hunaa min fadlik* اريد ان انزل هنا من فضلك
Go...	*Taharrak/idhhab* تحرك/اذهب
You have to go here	*Yajibu an tadhhaba min hunaa* يجب ان تذهب من هنا
Go straight ahead	*Idhhab mubaasharatan* اذهب مباشرة
Turn left	*In'atif ilaa l-yasaar* إنعطف الى اليسار
Turn right	*In'atif ilaa l-yamiin* إنعطف الى اليمين
This is it/We're here	*Haadhaa huwa l-'unwaan/laqad wasalnaa* هذا هو العنوان/لقد وصلنا
Could you wait a minute for me, please?	*Hal tantazirunii daqiiqa min fadlik?* هل تنتظرني دقيقة من فضلك؟

7 A Place to Stay

7. A Place to Stay

7.1 General

كم ستبقى هنا ؟	How long will you be staying?
املأ هذه الاستمارة من فضلك	Fill out this form, please
هل يمكن ان ارى جواز سفرك؟	Could I see your passport?
احتاج الى تسبقة	I'll need a deposit
عليك ان تدفع مقدما	You'll have to pay in advance

My name is...
Ismii...
اسمي...

I've made a reservation
Ladayya hajz
لدي حجز

How much is it per night/
week/month?
Kam ujrat l-layla/al-'usbuu'/ash-shahr?
كم اجرة الليلة/الأسبوع/الشهر ؟

We'll be staying at least...
nights/weeks
Sa-nabqaa 'alaa l-aqal...layaalin/ asaabii'
سنبقى على الاقل...ليال/اسابيع

We don't know yet
Ilaa haddi l'aan laa na'rif
الى حد الان لا نعرف

Do you allow pets (cats/
dogs)?
Hal tasmah bi-'istihaab haywaanaat aliifa?
هل تسمح باصطحاب حيوانات اليفة؟

What time does the gate/
door open/close?
Mataa taftah/tughliq al-bawaaba/ albaab?
متى تفتح/تغلق البوابة/الباب؟

Could you get me a taxi, please?	*Hal yumkin an tatluba lii taaksi min fadlik?*
	هل يمكن ان تطلب لي تاكسي من فضلك؟
Is there any mail for me?	*Hal hunaak ay bariid lii?*
	هل هناك اي بريد لي؟

7.2 Hotels/B&Bs/apartments/holiday rentals

Do you have a single/ double room available?	*Hal tatawaffar ladayka ghurfa lishakhs/lishakhsayn?*
	هل تتوفر لديك غرفة لشخص/لشخصين؟
– per person/per room	*lkul shakhs/likul ghurfa*
	لكل شخص/لكل غرفة
Does that include breakfast/lunch/dinner?	*Hal haadhaa yashmal al-iftaar/ al-ghadaa'/al-'ashaa'?*
	هل هذا يشمل الافطار/الغداء/العشاء؟
Could we have two adjoining rooms?	*Hal yumkin an nahsula 'alaa ghurfatayn mutajaawiratayn?*
	هل يمكن ان نحصل على غرفتين متجاوريتين؟
– with/without toilet/ bath/shower	*ma'a/biduun maraafiq/hammaam/ dush*
	مع/بدون مرافق/حمام/دش
– facing the street	*muwaajih lish-shaari'*
	مواجه للشارع
– at the back	*fii al-khalf*
	في الخلف
– with/without sea view	*ma'a/biduun itlaala 'alaa al-bahr*
	مع/بدون اطلالة على البحر
Is there...in the hotel?	*Hal yuujadu...fii al-funduq?*
	هل يوجد...في الفندق؟

الحمام والمرافق في نفس الطابق/ في الغرفة	The toilet and shower are on the same floor/in the room
من هنا من فضلك	This way, please
غرفتك في الطابق... ، رقم...	Your room is on the... floor, number...

Is there an elevator in the hotel?

Hal yuujadu mis'ad kahrabaa'ii fii al-funduq?

هل يوجد مصعد كهربائي في الفندق؟

Do you have room service?

Hal tuwaffir khadamaat lil-ghuraf?

هل توفر خدمات للغرف؟

Could I see the room?

Hal yumkin an araa al-ghurfa?

هل يمكن ان ارى الغرفة؟

I'll take this room

Sa-aakhudh haadhihi al-ghurfa

سآخذ هذه الغرفة

We don't like this one

Nahnu laa nuriidu haadha

نحن لا نريد هذا

Do you have a larger/less expensive room?

Hal ladayka ghurfa akbar/arkhas?

هل لديك غرفة اكبر/ارخص؟

Could you put in a cot?

Hal yumkin an tada'a sariir atfaal?

هل يمكن ان تضع سرير أطفال؟

What time's breakfast?

Mataa waqt al-'iftaar?

متى وقت الافطار؟

Where's the dining room?

Ayna ghurfat at-ta'aam?

اين غرفة الطعام؟

Can I have breakfast in my room?

Hal yumkin an atanaawala fatuurii fii ghurfatii?

هل يمكن ان اتناول فطوري في غرفتي؟

108

Where's the emergency exit/fire escape?	*Ayna makhraj at-tawaari'/manfadh al-hariiq?* اين مخرج الطواريء/منفذ الحريق؟
Where can I park my car safely?	*Ayna yumkin an uuqifa sayyaaratii?* أين يمكن ان أوقف سيارتي؟
The key to room..., please	*Miftaah al-ghurfa...min fadlik* مفتاح الغرفة...من فضلك
Could you put this in the safe, please?	*Hal yumkin an tahfaza lii haadha fii al-amaanaat?* هل يمكن ان تحفظ لي هذا في الامانات من فضلك؟
Could you wake me at... tomorrow?	*Hal yumkin an tuqizanii as-saa'a... ghadan?* هل يمكن ان توقظني الساعة...غدا؟
Could you find a babysitter for me?	*Hal yumkin an ahsula 'alaa murabbiyat atfaal?* هل يمكن ان احصل على مربية أطفال؟
Could I have an extra blanket?	*Hal yumkin an ahsula 'alaa battaniyya idaafiyya?* هل يمكن ان احصل على بطانية اضافية؟
What days do the cleaners come in?	*fii ay yawm ya'tii al-munazzifuun?* في أي يوم يأتي المنظفون؟
When are the sheets/ towels/dish towels changed?	*Mataa yatum taghyiir ash-sharaashif/ al-manaashif/manaashif al-hammaam?* متى يتم تغيير الشراشف/المناشف/ مناشف الحمام؟

7.3 Complaints

We can't sleep for the noise	*Laa nastatii' an nanaama bi-sababi al-dawdaa'* لا نستطيع ان ننام بسبب الضوضاء

Could you turn the radio down, please?	*Hal yumkin an takhfida' sawt al-midhyaa' (ar-raadiyuu) min fadlik?* هل يمكن ان تخفض صوت المذياع (الراديو) من فضلك؟
We're out of toilet paper	*Laa tuujad awraaq (kliiniks) fii attuwaaliit* لا توجد اوراق (كلينكس) في التواليت
There aren't any.../there's not enough...	*Laa yuujad hunaak ay.../laa yuujad... kaafii* لا يوجد هناك اي.../لا يوجد...كافي
The bed linen's dirty	*Aghtiyat al-firaash wasikha* أغطية الفراش وسخة
The room hasn't been cleaned	*Al-ghurfa lam tunazaf* الغرفة لم تنظف
The kitchen is not clean	*Al-matbakh laysa naziifan* المطبخ ليس نظيفا
The kitchen utensils are dirty	*Adawaat al-matbakh wasikha* أدوات المطبخ وسخة
The heating isn't working	*At-tadfi'a laa ta'mal* التدفئة لا تعمل
There's no hot water/ electricity	*Laa yuujad maa' saakhin/kahrabaa'* لا يوجد ماء ساخن/كهرباء
...doesn't work/is broken	*Al-...laa ya'mal/maksuur* ال...لا يعمل/مكسور
Could you have that seen too?	*Hal yumkin an tafhasa dhaalik aydan?* هل يمكن ان تفحص ذلك أيضا؟
Could I have another room/site?	*Hal ladayka ghurfa/mawqi' aakhar?* هل لديك غرفة/موقع اخر؟
The bed creaks terribly	*Al-firaash yusdiru sawtan muz'ijan* الفراش يصدر صوتا مزعجا

The bed sags	*Al-firaash yartakhii* الفراش يرتخي
Could I have a board under the mattress?	*Hal yumkin an tada'a khashaba tahta al-farsha?* هل يمكن ان تضع خشبة تحت الفرشة؟
It's too noisy	*Dawdaa' shdeeda* ضوضاء شديدة
There are a lot of insects	*Yuujad al-kathiir min al-hasharaat* يوجد الكثير من الحشرات
This place is full of mosquitoes	*Haadhaa al-makaan malii' bil-ba'uud* هذا المكان مليء بالبعوض
– cockroaches	*saraasiir* صراصير

A Place to Stay

7

7.4 Departure

See also 8.2 Settling the bill

I'm leaving tomorrow	*Sa-'ughaadir ghadan* سأغادر غدا
Could I pay my bill, please?	*Al-faatuura min fadlik?* الفاتورة من فضلك؟
What time should we check-out?	*Mataa yajibu an natruka al-ghurfa?* متى يجب أن نترك الغرفة؟
Could I have my deposit/ passport back, please?	*Hal yumkin an astarji'a ad-damaan/ jawaaza safarii min fadlik?* هل يمكن ان استرجع الضمان/ جواز سفري من فضلك؟
We're in a big hurry	*Nahnu musta'jiluuna jiddan* نحن مستعجلون جدا

Could you forward my mail to this address?	*Hal yumkin an tuhawwila bariiddii ilaa haadhaa al-'unwaan?* هل يمكن ان تحول بريدي الى هذا العنوان؟
Could we leave our luggage here until we leave?	*Hal yumkin an natruk haqaa'ibanaa hunaa ilaa hiin nughaadir?* هل يمكن ان نترك حقائبنا هنا الى حين نغادر؟
Thanks for your hospitality	*Shukran 'alaa husni ad-diyaafa* شكرا على حسن الضيافة

7.5 Camping

See the diagram on page 115

يمكن ان تختار الموقع الذي تريده	You can pick your own site
سنعطيك موقعا	You'll be allocated a site
هذا رقم موقعك	This is your site number
اربط هذا جيدا بسيارتك، من فضلك	Please stick this firmly to your car
يجب ان لا تفقد هذه البطاقة	You must not lose this card

Where's the manager?	*Ayna al-mudiir?* اين المدير؟
Are we allowed to camp here?	*Hal masmuuh an nukhayyima hunaa?* هل مسموح ان نخيم هنا؟
There are...of us and we have...tents	*Nahnu...afraad, wa ladaynaa... khiyam* نحن...افراد، ولدينا...خيم
Can we pick our own site?	*Hal yumkin an nakhtaara al-mawqi'a alladhii nuriid?* هل يمكن ان نختار الموقع الذي نريد؟

Do you have a quiet spot for us?	*Hal ladayka makaan haadi' lanaa?* هل لديك مكان هاديء لنا؟
Do you have any other sites available?	*Hal tatawaffar ladayka mawaaqi' ukhraa?* هل تتوفر لديك مواقع اخرى؟
It's too crowded here	*Haadhaa l-makaanu muzdahim jiddan* هذا المكان مزدحم جدا
It's too windy/sunny/ shady here.	*Riih shadiida/shams qawiyya/zil kathiif/hunaa* ريح شديدة/شمس قوية/ظل كثيف/هنا
The ground's too hard/ uneven	*Al-ard salba jiddan/muta'arrija* الارض صلبة جدا/متعرجة
Do you have a level spot for the trailer?	*Hal ladayka makaan lil-'araba?* هل لديك مكان للعربة؟
Could we have adjoining sites?	*Hal yumkin an nahsula 'alaa mawaaqi'a mutaqaariba?* هل يمكن ان نحصل على مواقع متقاربة؟
Can we park the car next to the tent?	*Hal yumkin an nuuqifa as-sayyaara qurba al-khayma?* هل يمكن ان نوقف السيارة قرب الخيمة؟
How much is it per person/tent/trailer/car?	*Kam al-ujra lil-fard al-waahid/ lil-khayma/lil-'araba/lis-sayyaara?* كم الاجرة للفرد الواحد/للخيمة/ للعربة/للسيارة؟
Do you have chalets for hire?	*Hal ladayka bayt istiyaaf lil-'iijaar?* هل لديك بيت اصطياف للإيجار؟
Are there any...?	*Hal hunaaka ay...?* هل هناك اي...؟
– hot showers	*dush saakhin* دش ساخن؟

Camping equipment

(The diagram shows the numbered parts)

	luggage space	مكان الحقائب	makaan al-haqaa'iib
	can opener	مفتاح علب	miftaah 'ulab
	butane gas	غاز البوتان	ghaaz al-buutaan
	bottle	زجاجة	zujaja
1	pannier	سلة كبيرة	salla kabiira
2	gas cooker	جهاز طهي	jihaaz tahiy
3	groundsheet	غطاء الارض	ghitaa' al-ard
	hammer	مطرقة	mitraqa
	hammock	ارجوحة شبكية	urjuuha shabakiyya
4	gas can	علبة غاز	'ulbat ghaaz
	campfire	نار المخيم	naar al-mukhayyam
5	folding chair	كرسي قابل للطوي	kursi qaabil lit-tawii
6	insulated picnic box	صندوق عازل	sunduuq aazil
	ice pack	كيس ثلج	kiis thalj
	compass	بوصلة	bawsala
	corkscrew	مفتاح قناني	miftaah qanaani
7	airbed	الفراش الهوائي	al-firaash al-hawaa'iy
8	airbed pump	منفاخ الفراش الهوائي	minfaakh al-firaash al-hawaa'iy
9	awning	مظلة	mizalla
10	sleeping bag	حقيبة نوم	haqiibat nawm
11	saucepan	قدر صغير	qidr saghiir
12	handle (pan)	اليد الماسكة	al-yad al-maasika
	primus stove	جهاز طهي صغير	jihaaz tahiy saghiir
	lighter	ولاعة/قداحة	walla'a/qaddaha
13	backpack	حقيبة ظهر	haqiibat zahr
14	guy rope	حبل	habl
15	storm lantern	مصباح العاصفة	misbaah al-'aasifa
	camp bed	فراش مخيم	firaash mukhayyam
	table	طاولة	taawila
16	tent	خيمة	khayma
17	tent peg	وتد الخيمة	watad al-khayma
18	tent pole	عمود الخيمة	'amuud al-khayma
	thermos	ترمس	tarmus
19	water bottle	قنينة ماء	qinniinat maa'
	clothes pin	مساك ملابس	massaak malaabis
	clothes line	حبل الغسيل	habl al-ghasiil
	windbreak	واقية من الريح	waaqiya min ar-riih
20	flashlight	ضوء وامض	daw' waamid
	penknife	سكين قلم	sikkiin qalam

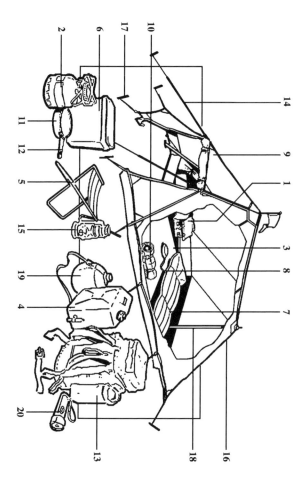

– washing machines	*ghassaala* غسالة
Is there a...on the site?	*Hal yuujad...fii haadhaa al-makaan?* هل يوجد...في هذا المكان؟
Is there a children's play area on the site?	*Hal tuujad saahat la'ib lil-atfaal fii haadhaa al-makaan?* هل توجد ساحة لعب للاطفال في هذا المكان؟
Are there covered cooking facilities on the site?	*hal tuujad tashiilat tabkh mughattaat fii haadhaa al-makaan?* هل توجد تسهيلات طبخ مغطاة في هذا المكان؟
Can I rent a safe?	*hal yumkin an asta'jjira sunduuq amaanaat?* هل يمكن ان استأجر صندوق امانات؟
Are we allowed to barbecue here?	*hal yusmahu lanaa an nashwiya hunaa?* هل يسمح لنا ان نشوي هنا؟
Are there any power outlets?	*hal tuujad manaafidha kahrubaa'iyya?* هل توجد منافذ كهربائية؟
Is there drinking water?	*hal yuujad maa' shurb?* هل يوجد ماء شرب؟
When's the garbage collected?	*mataa yatim jam' az-zibaala?* متى يتم جمع الزبالة؟
Do you sell gas bottles (butane gas/propane gas)?	*hal tabii' qanaani ghaaz?* هل تبيع قناني غاز؟

8 Money Matters

8. Money Matters

● In general, banks are open to the public from 8.30 a.m. to 12.30 p.m., and 1.30 to 4.30 p.m., but it is always possible to find an exchange office (*masraf*) open in larger towns or tourist centers. Proof of identity is usually required to exchange currency. Keep in mind that Friday, not Sunday, is the day off in most countries of the Middle East.

8.1 Banks

Where can I find a bank/ an exchange office around here?	*Ayna yumkin an ajida maṣrafan/ maktab taghyeer 'umla ajnabiyya hunaa?* اين يمكن ان اجد مصرفا/مكتب تغيير عملة أجنبية هنا ؟
Where can I cash this traveler's check?	*Ayna yumkin an aṣrifa haadhaa ash-shiik?* اين يمكن ان اصرف هذا الشيك؟
Can I cash this here?	*Hal yumkin an asrifa haadhaa hunaa?* هل يمكن ان أصرف هذا هنا ؟
Can I withdraw money on my credit card here?	*Hal yumkin an aṣhaba ba'da an-nuquud hunaa bi-waasiṭati biṭaaqat al-i'timaad?* هل يمكن ان اسحب بعض النقود هنا بواسطة بطاقة الاعتماد ؟
What's the minimum/ maximum amount?	*Maa huwa aqṣaa/adnaa mablagh?* ما هو اقصى/ادنى مبلغ؟
Can I take out less than that?	*Hal astaṭii'u an aṣhaba aqalla min dhaalik?* هل استطيع ان اسحب اقل من ذلك؟

I had some money cabled here	*Laqad ursila mablagh maaliy li-hisaabii ilaa hunaa* لقد ارسل مبلغ مالي لحسابي الى هنا
Has it arrived yet?	*Hal wasala ba'du?* هل وصل بعد؟
These are the details of my bank in the USA	*Haadhihi tafaasiil masrafii fii amriika* هذه تفاصيل مصرفي في امريكا
This is the number of my bank/account	*Haadhaa raqmu masrafii/raqmu hisaabii* هذا رقم مصرفي/رقم حسابي
I'd like to change some money	*Uriid an uhawwila (usarrifa) ba'da an-nuquud* اريد ان احول (اصرف) بعض النقود
– pounds into...	*min al-jiniih ilaa...* من الجنيه إلى...
– dollars into...	*min ad-duulaar ilaa...* من الدولار إلى...

وقع هنا من فضلك	Sign here, please
املأ هذا من فضلك	Fill this out, please
هل يمكن أن أرى جواز سفرك من فضلك؟	Could I see your passport, please?
هل يمكن ان ارى بطاقتك الشخصية من فضلك؟	Could I see your identity card, please?
هل يمكن ان ارى بطاقة التثبت من فضلك؟	Could I see your check card, please?
هل استطيع ان ارى بطاقتك المصرفية من فضلك؟	Could I see your bank card, please?

What's the exchange rate?	*Maa huwa si'ru al-'umla?* ما هو سعر العملة؟
Could you give me some small change with it?	*Hal yumkin an tu'tiyanii ba'd al-fakka ma'a haadha?* هل يمكن ان تعطيني بعض الفكة مع هذا؟

8.2 Settling the bill

Could you put it on my bill?	*Hal yumkin an tudiifahu ilaa al-faatuura?* هل يمكن ان تضيفه الى الفاتورة؟
Is the tip included?	*Hal ikraamiyya (al-baqshiish) dimn as-si'r?* هل الإكرامية (البقشيش) ضمن السعر؟
Can I pay by...?	*Hal yumkin an adfa'a bi-waasitati...?* هل يمكن ان ادفع بواسطة...؟
Can I pay by credit card?	*Hal yumkin an adfa'a bi-waasitati bitaaqat i'timaad?* هل يمكن ان ادفع بواسطة بطاقة اعتماد؟
Can I pay by traveler's check?	*Hal asatii' ad-daf' bi-waasitati shiik siyaahii?* هل استطيع الدفع بواسطة شيك سياحي؟
Can I pay with foreign currency?	*Hal yumkin an adfa'a bil-'umla al-ajnabiyya?* هل يمكن ان ادفع بالعملة الاجنبية؟
You've given me too much/you haven't given me enough change	*A'ttaytanii kathiiran/lam tu'ttinii kul al-baaqii* اعطيتني كثيرا/لم تعطني كل الباقي
Could you check this again, please?	*Hal yumkin an tatathabbata marratan uhkhraa?* هل يمكن ان تتثبت مرة اخرى؟

Could I have a receipt, please?
Hal yumkin an ahsula 'alaa wasl?
هل يمكن ان احصل على وصل؟

I don't have enough money on me
Laysa ma'ii nuquud kaafiya
ليس معي نقود كافية

نحن لا نقبل بطاقات الاعتماد/
شيك سياحي/عملات اجنبية
We don't accept credit cards/ traveler's checks/ foreign currency

---

This is for you
Haadhaa laka
هذا لك

Keep the change
Ihtafiz bil-baaqii
احتفظ بالباقي

8.3 Business terms

I work online
Anaa a'mal 'alaa al-net
أنا أعمل على النت

I have experience
'Indii khibra
عندي خبرة

Is the manager here?
Hal al mudiir maujuud?
هل المدير موجود؟

I want to meet the owner of the company?
Uriidu an uqaabila Saahib al-sharika
أريد أن أقابل صاحب الشركة

Can I send the contract by e-mail?
Hal yumkin an ursila al-'aqd bibariid iliktoronii?
هل يمكن أن أرسل العقد بالبريد الألكتروني؟

How much will my salary be?
Kam sayakuun raatibii?
كم سيكون راتبي؟

شركة	رجل أعمال
sharika	**rajulu a'maal**
company	businessman

استيراد	سيدة أعمال
istiraad	**saiyidat a'maal**
importation	businesswoman

تصدير	صاحب الشركة
tasdiir	**saahib al-sharika**
export	owner of the company

مدير	شركة متعددة الجنسيات
mudiir	**sharikatun muta'addidat al-jinsiyaat**
manager	multinational corporation

سيرة ذاتية	محترف – مهني / محترفة – مهنية
sira dhaatiya	**muhtarif-mihani/muhtarifa-mihaniya**
resume/CV	professional (m/f)

شهادة	متخصص / متخصصة
shihaada	**mutakhassis/mutakhassisa**
certificate	specialist (m/f)

عقد	مؤهل / مؤهلة
'aqd	**mu'ahhal/mu'ahhal**
contract	qualified (m/f)

وظيفة	درجة الماجستير
waziifa	**darajat al-maajistiir**
job	master's degree

راتب	خبير / خبيرة
raatib	**khibiir/khibiira**
salary	expert (m/f)

9 Mail, Phone and Internet

9. Mail, Phone and Internet

9.1 Mail

For banks, see 8 Money matters

● Major post offices are open Sunday to Thursday from 8.30 a.m. to 5.00 p.m. Stamps (*tawaabi'*) can also be purchased at authorized tobacconists (*dukkaan*). The cost of sending a letter depends on its weight and the cost of sending an airmail letter also depends on where it is being sent. Postal services in some countries in the Middle East are quite slow.

طوابع	رزم	برقيات	حوالة بريدية
ṯawaabi'	*ruzam*	*barqiyyaat*	*ḥawaala bariidiyya*
stamps	parcels	telegrams	money orders

Where is...?	*Ayna...?*
	اين...
– the nearest post office	*aqrab maktab bariid*
	أقرب مكتب بريد
– the main post office	*maktab al-bariid ar-ra'iisii*
	مكتب البريد الرئيسي
– the nearest mail box	*aqrab ṣunduuq bariid*
	أقرب صندوق بريد
Which counter should I go to?	*Ilaa ay shubbaak yajibu an adh'haba li?*
	الى اي شباك يجب ان اذهب ل؟
Which counter should I go to to send a fax?	*Ilaa ay shubbaak yajibu an adh'haba li'irsaal faaks?*
	الى اي شباك يجب ان اذهب لإرسال فاكس؟
Which counter should I go to to change money?	*Ilaa ay shubbaak yajibu an adh'haba li taghyeer umla?*
	إلى أي شباك يجب أن أذهب لتغيير عملة؟

Which counter should I go to to change giro checks?	*Ilaa ay shubbaak yajibu an adh'haba li-tasriif haadhaa ash-shiik?* الى اي شباك يجب ان اذهب لتصريف هذا الشيك؟
Which counter should I go to to cash this check?	*Ilaa ay shubbaak yajibu an adh'haba lisarf hadhaa ash-shiik?* الى اي شباك يجب ان لصرف هذا الشيك؟
Which counter should I go to for general delivery?	*Ilaa ay shubbaak yajibu an adh'haba li-tasallum al-amti'a?* الى اي شباك يجب ان اذهب لتسلم الأمتعة
Is there any mail for me?	*Hal yuujad ay bariid lii?* هل يوجد اي بريد لي
My name's...	*Ismii...* اسمي...

Stamps

What's the postage for a... to...?	*Kam ujrat al-bariid li...laa...?* كم أجرة البريد ل...ال...
Are there enough stamps on it?	*Hal fiihaa tawaabi' kaafiya?* هل فيها طوابع كافية؟
I'd like [quantity] [value] stamps	*Uriidu maa qiimatuhu...tawaabi'...* اريد ما قيمته...طوابع...
I'd like to send this...	*Uriidu an ursila haadhihi...* اريد ان ارسل هذه...
– by express	*bi-lbariid as-sarii'* بالبريد السريع
– by air mail	*bi-lbariid al-jawwii* بالبريد الجوي
– by registered mail	*bi-lbariid al-musajjal* بالبريد المسجل

Telegram/fax

I'd like to send a telegram to...	*Uriidu an ursila barqiyya ilaa...* اريد ان ارسل برقية الى...
How much is that per word?	*Kam kulfatu kull kalima?* كم كلفة كل كلمة؟
This is the text I want to send	*Haadhaa huwa an-nas alladhii uriidu an ursilahu* هذا هو النص الذي اريد ان ارسله
Shall I fill out the form myself?	*Hal amla'u al-istimaara binafsii?* هل املأ الاستمارة بنفسي؟
Can I make photocopies/ send a fax here?	*Hal yumkin an usawwira wathaa'iqa (futukuubi)/ursil faaks min hunaa?* هل يمكن ان اصور وثائق (فوتوكوبي) / ارسل فاكس من هنا؟
How much is it per page?	*Kam kulfat kull safha?* كم كلفة كل صفحة؟

9.2 Telephone

See also 1.9 Telephone alphabets

● Direct internasional calls can easily be made from public telephones using a phone card available from newspaper stands, and post offices and Telecom offices. Dial 00 to get out of the country, then the relevant country code (USA 1), city code and number. Collect phone calls are difficult to make and the fact that many operators do not speak English makes them even more inaccessible. When phoning someone in an Arab country, you will be greeted with "*aaluu*".

Is there a phone booth around here?	*Hal yuujad haatif 'umuumii qariib min hunaa?* هل يوجد هاتف عمومي قريب من هنا؟

May I use your phone, please?	*Hal yumkin an astakhdima haatifak?* هل يمكن ان استخدم هاتفك؟
Do you have a city phone directory?	*Hal ladayka daliil bi'arqaam hawaatif al-madiina?* هل لديك دليل بأرقام هواتف المدينة؟
Where can I get a phone card?	*Ayna yumkin an ahsula 'alaa bitaaqat tilifuun?* اين يمكن ان احصل على بطاقة تلفون؟
Could you give me…?	*Hal yumkin an tu'tiyanii…?* هل يمكن ان تعطيني...؟
– the number for international directory assistance	*raqm al-musaa'da ad-duwalii* رقم المساعدة الدولي
– the room number…	*raqm ghurfa…* رقم غرفة...
– the international access code	*al-miftaah ad-duwalii* المفتاح الدولي
– the country code for…	*miftaah al-balad…* مفتاح البلد...
– the area code for…	*miftaah al-mintaqa…* مفتاح المنطقة...
– the number of… [subscriber]	*raqamu al-mushtarik…* رقم المشترك...
Could you check if this number's correct?	*Hal yumkin an ta-ta'akkada anna haadhaa ar-raqm sahiih?* هل يمكن ان تتأكد ان هذا الرقم صحيح؟
Can I dial international direct?	*Hal astatii'u an attasila bil-khaarij mubaasharatan?* هل أستطيع ان اتصل بالخارج مباشرة؟
Do I have to reserve my calls?	*Hal yajibu an ahjiza mukaalamaatii?* هل يجب ان احجز مكالماتي؟

Do I have to go through the switchboard?	*Hal yajibu an attaṣila awwalan bi-markazi al-ittiṣaalaat?* هل يجب ان أتصل أولا بمركز الإتصالات؟
Do I have to dial 0 first?	*Hal yajibu an udawwira ar-raqm 0 awwalan?* هل يجب ان ادور الرقم 0 أولا؟
Could you dial this number for me, please?	*Laa samaḥt hal yumkin an taṭluba lii haadhaa ar-raqm?* لو سمحت هل يمكن ان تطلب لي هذا الرقم؟
Could you put me through to.../extension..., please?	*Hal yumkin an tuhawwilanii 'alaa.../ ar-raqam ad-dakhilii...min faḍlik?* هل يمكن ان تحولني على.../ الرقم الداخلي...من فضلك؟
I'd like to place a collect call to...	*Uriidu an aquuma bi-mukaalama ilaa...'alaa ḥisaab al-mustalim* اريد ان اقوم بمكالمة الى...على حساب المستلم
What's the charge per minute?	*Kam kulfat ad-daqiiqa al-waaḥida?* كم كلفة الدقيقة الواحدة؟
Have there been any calls for me?	*Hal wasalatnii mukaalamaat haatifiyya?* هل وصلتني مكالمات هاتفية؟

محمول/جوال *maḥmoul/jawwal* cell phone	شاحن السيارة *shaaḥin al-saiyara* car charger	بطارية *baṭṭariya* battery
هاتف ذكي *hatif dhakii* smartphone	بطاقة شحن الرصيد *biṭaqat shaḥn al-raṣiid* phone card	شاحن *shaaḥin* charger
خط جديد *khat jadiid* New line	مكتب اتصالات (سنترال) *maktab ittisalat (sentiral)* calling office	

The conversation

Hello, this is...	*Aaluu ma'aka...* ...آلو معك
Who is this, please?	*Man 'alaa l-khat?* من على الخط؟
Is this...?	*Hal haadha...?* هل هذا...؟
I'm sorry, I've dialed the wrong number	*Anaa aasif, talabtu raqman khata'* انا آسف طلبت رقما خطأ
I can't hear you	*Laa astatii'u an asma'aka* لا استطيع ان اسمعك
I'd like to speak to...	*Uriidu an atakallama ma'a...* ...اريد ان أتكلم مع
Is there anybody who speaks English?	*Hal yuujad ay shakhs yatakallam al-inkliiziyya?* هل يوجد اي شخص يتكلم الانكليزية؟
Extension..., please	*Ar-raqm ad-daakhilii...min fadlik* الرقم الداخلي...من فضلك
Could you ask him/her to call me back?	*Hal yumkin an tatluba minhu an yattasila/hal yumkin an tatluba minhaa an tattasila bii?* هل يمكن ان تطلب منه ان يتصل/هل يمكن ان تطلب منها أن تتصل بي؟
My name's...	*Ismii...* ...اسمي
My number's...	*Raqmii huwa...* ...رقمي هو
Could you tell him/her I called?	*Hal yumkin an tukhbirahu/tukhbirahaa annii ittasaltu?* هل يمكن ان تخبره/تخبرها اني اتصلت؟

I'll call him/her back
  tomorrow

Sawfa attasil bihi/bihaa ghadan
سوف أتصل به/بها غدا

هناك مكالمة هاتفية لك	There's a phone call for you
يجب ان تدور الرقم 0 أولا	You have to dial 0 first
لحظة من فضلك	One moment, please
ليس هناك من يرد	There's no answer
الخط مشغول	The line's busy
هل تريد ان تبقى على الخط؟	Do you want to hold?
احولك إلى	Connecting you
طلبت رقما خطأ	You've got a wrong number
هو غير موجود/هي غير موجودة في الوقت الحاضر	He's/she's not here right now
هو سيعود/هي ستعود الساعة...	He'll/she'll be back at...
هذا جهاز الرد الآلي...	This is the answering machine of...

9.3 Internet/email

● Internet is available in the Arab world. Hot spots are available in various places like hotels, coffee shops and some restaurants. Also, you can go to an Internet café for a direct and quick access. Internet terminology is pretty much the same as in English. Plus you will find a lot of people who speak English in case you need help. Thanks to the social media revolution, people are well connected around the world.

What is your e-mail?

Maa Bariiduka al-iliktoronii?
ما بريدك الأكتروني؟

حاسوب محمول **hasoub mahmoul** laptop	تحميل **tahmiil** download	بريد إلكتروني **bariid iliktoronii** e-mail	إنترنت **Internet** Internet
شبكات التواصل الاجتماعي **shabakaat al-tawasul al-ijtimaa'ii** social networks	ثتبيت **tathbiit** install	محرك بحث **muharrik bahth** web browser	فيروس **fairoos** virus
	كاميرا **kamira** webcam	كلمة السر **kalimat al-ser** password	فايس بوك **Facebook** Facebook
مقهي إنترنت (سايبر) **maqha internet (saybar)** Internet café (cyber)	طابعة **tabi'a** printer	محادثة **muhadatha** chat	تويتر **Twitter** Twitter
البريد غير المرغوب فيه **al-bariid ghiir marghoub fiih** junk mail	بحث **bahth** search	ماسح ضوئي **masiih daw'ii** scanner	

Do you have an account on ….?	*Hal laka hisaab "ala…?* هل لك حساب على...؟
Do you use ….?	*Hal tastakhdim…?* هل تستخدم...؟
Do you have this program in your computer?	*Hal 'indaka hadha al-barnamij "ala hasoubak?* هل عندك هذا البرنامج على حاسوبك؟
I sent a message to you	*Arsaltu laka risaala* أرسلت لك رسالة
I am on line	*Ana 'ala al-khat* أنا على الخط
I lost the connection	*Inqata'a al-khat* انقطع الخط
The Internet is slow	*Al-internet batii'* الأنترنت بطيء

10 Shopping

10. Shopping

• Shops are generally open Saturday to Thursday from 9.00 a.m. to 7.30 p.m. Grocery shops may not re-open until 5.00 p.m. and could stay open until 9.00 p.m. in the summer. Shops, department stores and supermarkets usually close for a half day during the week – usually on Friday afternoons. Some variation across countries also exists as to the hours of business.

دكان بقالة
dukkaan baqaala
grocery shop

حلاق
hallaaq
barber's

جزار
jazzaar
butcher's shop

دكان احذية
dukkaan ahdhiya
footwear

اسكافي
iskaafii
cobbler

سوق
suuq
market

بضائع منزلية
badaa'i' manziliyya
household goods

بائع الدواجن
baa'i' ad-dawaajin
poultry shop

محل آلي لتنظيف الملابس
mahal aalii li-tanziif al-malaabis
coin-operated laundry/dry cleaner

دكان لبيع الكتب
dukkaan libay' al-kutub
bookshop

مجوهرات أزياء
mujawharaat azyaa'
costume jewelry

ورشة تصليح دراجات
warshat tasliih darraajaat
motorbike and bicycle repairs

دكان قرطاسية
dukkaan qurtaasiyyya
stationery shop

محل لوازم الخياطة
mahal lawaazim al-khiyaata
haberdashery

محل خضار وفواكه
mahal khudaar wa fawaakih
fruit and vegetable shop

دكان الات موسيقية
dukkaan aalaat muusiiqiyya
musical instrument shop

وكالة طباعة
wikaalat tibaa'a
typing agency

دكان اخدم نفسك بنفسك
dukkaan ikhdim nafsak binafsik
do-it-yourself shop

كشك لبيع الصحف
kushk li bay' as-suhuf
newsstand

دكان مجوهرات
dukkaan mujawharaat
goldsmith

مخزن خمور
makhzan khumuur
stock of vintage wines

دكان بضاعة مستعملة
dukkaan bidaa'a musta'mala
second-hand shop

دكان ملابس
dukkaan malaabis
clothing shop

دكان ادوية الاعشاب
dukkaan adwiat al-a'shaab
herbalist's shop

صيدلية
saydaliyya
pharmacy

دكان لوازم مخيم
dukkaan lawaazim mukhayyam
camping supplies shop

بائع الورد
baa'i' al-ward
florist

دكان آلات التصوير
dukkaan aalaat at-taswiir
telecoms shop

خباز
khabbaaz
bakery

لوازم رياضية
lawaazim riyaadiyya
sporting goods

بائع الخضار
baai'i' al-khudar
greengrocer

دكان الشراشف
dukkaan ash-sharaashif
household linen shop

ساعاتي
saa'aatii
watches and clocks

محل اشرطة موسيقية
mahall ashrita muusiqiyya
music shop (CDs, tapes, etc.)

النظاراتي
an-nazzaaraatii
optician

دكان حلويات
dukkaan halawiyyaat
confectioner's/cake shop

مخبزة
makhbaza
baker's shop

السوق المركزية
as-suuq al-markaziyya
supermarket

دكان بوظة	لوازم منزلية
dukkaan buuza	*lawaazim manziliyah*
ice-cream shop	household appliances (white goods)

صائغ	دكان غسل ملابس
saa'igh	*dukkaan ghasl malaabis*
jeweler	laundry

مشتل	دكان مشتقات الحليب
mashtal	*dukkaan mushtaqqaat l-haliib*
nursery (plants)	dairy (shop selling dairy products)

صالون تجميل	المخزن الرئيسي
saaluun tajmiil	*al-makhzan ar-ra'iissi*
beauty salon	department store

حلاق	دكان لبيع اللعب
hallaaq	*dukkaan libay' al-lu'ab*
hairdresser	toy shop

لوازم جلدية	بائع العطور
lawaazim jildiyyah	*baa'i' al-'utuur*
leather goods	perfumery

الفرائي	دكان معلبات
al-farraa'ii	*dukkaan mu'allabaat*
electronics shop	delicatessen

بائع السمك	كشك سجائر
baa'i' as-samak	*kushik sajaa'ir*
fishmonger	tobacconist

10.1 Shopping conversations

Where can I get...?	*Ayna ajidu...?*
	أين أجد...؟
When is this shop open?	*Mataa yaftahu haadhaa ad-dukkaan?*
	متى يفتح هذا الدكان؟

مهرجان التسوق	the Shopping Festival (annual month-long event held in Dubai)
شعار المهرجان	the festival symbol (used each year as a symbol of the Dubai Shopping Festival)
جنة التسوق	shopping paradise

How can I go to Dubai?
Kaifa adh'hab ilaa dubai
كيف أذهب إلى دبي؟

You can rent a car
Yumkin an tasta'jir sayyaara
يمكن أن تستأجر سيارة

You can take a taxi
Yumkin an ta'khudh taaksi
يمكن أن تأخذ تاكسي

Could you tell me where the...department is?
Hal tadullunii 'an mawqi'i qism al...?
هل تدلني عن موقع قسم...؟

Could you help me, please?
Min fadlik, hal tusaa'idunii 'alaa?
من فضلك، هل تساعدني على؟

I'm looking for...
Anaa abhathu 'an...
انا ابحث عن...

Do you sell English/ American newspapers?
Hal tabii' suhuf inkiliiziyya/ amariikiyya?
هل تبيع صحف انكليزية/امريكية؟

مركز تجاري	أربعون في المائة	ضريبة المبيعات
markaz tujari	**arba'uun**	**dariibat al-mabii'aat**
mall	40%	sales tax
تخفيض	ضرائب	
takhfiiad	**daraa'ib**	
discount	taxes	

There are many stores in the mall	*Fii al-markaz al-tujari mehallat kathirah* في المركز التجاري محلات كثيرة
The prices are expensive	*Alas'ar ghaliyah* الأسعار غالية
Are there discounts?	*Hal hunaak takhfiiadat* هل هناك تخفيضات؟
Are these prices without taxes?	*Hal al-as'aar biduun daraa'ib?* هل الأسعار بدون ضرائب؟
The tax will be returned to you at the airport	*Saufa tastarid al-Dariibah fii al-mataar* سوف تسترد الضريبة في المطار

هل يوجد من يخدمك؟   Are you being served?

No, I'd like...	*Laa, anaa arghabu fii...* لا انا ارغب في...
I'm just looking, if that's all right	*Anaa ulqii nazra faqat, hal fii maani'* انا ألقي نظرة فقط، هل في مانع

هل تطلب اي شيء اخر؟   Would you like anything else?

Yes, I'd also like...	*Na'am, uriidu aydan...* نعم اريد ايضا...
No thank you, that's all	*Laa shukran, haadhaa kul maa uriid* لا شكرا، هذا كل ما اريد
Could you show me...?	*Hal turiinii...?* هل تريني...؟

I'd prefer...	*Anaa ufaddil...* ...أنا افضل
This is not what I'm looking for	*Laysa haadhaa maa uriid* ليس هذا ما أريد
Thank you, I'll keep looking	*Shukran, sa-'uwaasil l-bahth* شكرا سأواصل البحث
Do you have something...?	*Hal ladayka bidaa'atan'...?* هل لديك بضاعة...؟
– less expensive	*arkhas* أرخص
– smaller/larger	*asghar/akbar* اصغر / اكبر
I'll take this one	*Sa-'aakhudhu haadha* سآخذ هذا
Does it come with instructions?	*Hal tuujadu ta'liimaat?* هل توجد تعليمات؟
It's too expensive	*Ghaalin jiddan* غال جدا
I'll give you...	*Sa-u'tiika...* ...سأعطيك
Could you keep this for me?	*Hal tahfaz haadha lii?* هل تحفظ هذا لي؟
I'll come back for it later	*Sawfa a-'uud fiimaa ba'd* سوف اعود فيما بعد
Do you have a bag for me, please?	*Hal ladayka haqiiba lii min fadlik?* هل لديك حقيبة لي من فضلك؟
Could you gift-wrap it, please?	*Hal yumkin an tughallifahaa lii min fadlik?* هل يمكن ان تغلفها لي من فضلك

انا اسف، ليس لدينا ذلك	I'm sorry, we don't have that
آسف بعنا ما لدينا	I'm sorry, we're sold out
اسف لن تكون لدينا حتى	I'm sorry, it won't come back in until...
من فضلك، ادفع لدى أمين الصندوق	Please pay at the cash register
لا نقبل بطاقات الاعتماد	We don't accept credit cards
لا نقبل شيك سياحي	We don't accept traveler's checks
لا نقبل عملات اجنبية	We don't accept foreign currency

10.2 Food

I'd like a hundred grams of..., please
Uriidu mi'at ghraam min...min fadlik
اريد مئة غرام من...من فضلك

I'd like half a kilo/five hundred grams of...
Uriidu nisf kiilu min...
اريد نصف كيلو من...

I'd like a kilo of...
Uriidu kiilughraaman min...
اريد كيلوغرام من...

Could you...it for me, please?
Hal yumkin an...lii min fadlik?
هل يمكن ان...لي من فضلك؟

– slice it/cut it up for me, please
qatt'ihaa/ij'alhaa sharaa'ih min fadlik
قطعها/اجعلها شرائح من فضلك

– grate it for me, please
qatt'ihaa ilaa qita' saghiira min fadlik
قطعها الى قطع صغيرة، من فضلك

Can I order it?
Hal yumkin an atluba?
هل يمكن ان اطلب؟

I'll pick it up tomorrow/ at...
Sawfa akhudhuhu ghadan/as-sa'aa...
سوف أخذه غدا/الساعة...

| Can you eat/drink this? | Hal yumkin an ta'kula/tashraba haadhaa?
هل يمكن ان تأكل/تشرب هذا ؟ |
|---|---|
| What's in it? | Maadhaa fiihi?
ماذا فيه؟ |

10.3 Clothing and shoes

حذاء	حذاء رياضي	رباط العنق	معطف
hidhaa'	hidhaa' riyadi	ribaat al-'unuq	mi'taf
shoe	athletic shoe	tie	overcoat
جورب	الفستان قصير	جورب أبيض	
jaurab	al-fustaan qasiir	jaurab abyad	
sock	short dress	white sock	

| I saw something in the window | Ra'aytu shay'an fii ash-shubbaak
رايت شيئا في الشباك |
|---|---|
| Shall I point it out? | Hal yumkin an ushiira ilaa dhaalika?
هل يمكن ان أشير إلى ذلك؟ |
| I'd like something to go with this | Uriidu shay'an yatanaasab ma'a haadha
اريد شيئا يتناسب مع هذا |
| I want a blue shirt | Uriidu qamiisan azraq
أريد قميصا أزرق |
| Do you have shoes to match this? | Hal ladayka hidhaa' yunaasib haadha
هل لديك حذاء يناسب هذا ؟ |
| I'm a size...in the USA | Anaa hijmii...fii al-qiyaas al-amariikii
انا حجمي...في القياس الأمريكي |
| Can I try this on? | Hal yumkin an ujarriba haadhaa?
هل يمكن ان اجرب هذا ؟ |

Where's the fitting room?	*Ayna ghurfat al-qiyaas?* اين غرفة القياس؟
It doesn't suit me	*Innahu laa yunaasibunii* انه لا يناسبني
It is big	*Innahu waasi'* إنه واسع
It is small	*Innahu daiyiq* أنه ضيق
The skirt is too long	*Al-tannuura tawiil* التنورة طويلة جدا
This is the right size	*Haadhaa huwa al-hajm al-munaasib* هذا هو الحجم المناسب
Do you have this/these in...?	*Hal ladayka haadhaa/haadhihi fii...?* هل لديك هذا/هذه في..؟
The heel's too high/low	*Al-ka'b 'aalin/munkhafid jiddan* الكعب عال/منخفض جدا
Is this real leather?	*Hal haadha jild haqiiqii?* هل هذا جلد حقيقي
Is this genuine hide?	*Hal haadha jild hayawaan haqiiqii?* هل هذا جلد حيوان حقيقي
I'm looking for a...for a... -year-old child	*Anaa abhath 'an...litifl 'umruhu...* أنا أبحث عن...لطفل عمره...
I'd like a...	*Uriidu* أريد...
– silk	*hariir* حرير
– cotton	*qutun* قطن
– woolen	*suufi* صوفي

| – linen | *kittaan* |
| | كتان |

| At what temperature should I wash it? | *Maa hiya darajat al-haraara al-munaasiba li-ghaslihi?* |
| | ما هي درجة الحرارة المناسبة لغسله؟ |

| Will it shrink in the wash? | *Hal yataqallas 'inda al-ghasl?* |
| | هل يتقلص عند الغسل؟ |

غسل يدوي	قابل للغسل بالغسالة	لا تكوي
ghasl yadawi	*qaabil lil-ghasl bil-ghassala*	*laa takwii*
Hand wash	Machine washable	Do not iron
تنظيف جاف	لا تجفف بالدوران السريع	ابسط
tanziif jaaf	*laa tujaffif bid-dawaraan as-sarii'*	*ibsit*
Dry clean	Do not spin dry	Lay flat

At the cobbler

| Could you mend these shoes? | *Hal yumkin an tusliha haadha al-hidhaa'?* |
| | هل يمكن أن تصلح هذا الحذاء؟ |

| Could you resole and reheel these shoes? | *Hal yumkin an tughayyira ka'b haadha l-hidhaa'?* |
| | هل يمكن أن تغير كعب هذا الحذاء؟ |

| When will they be ready? | *Mataa takuun jaahiza?* |
| | متى تكون جاهزة؟ |

| I'd like..., please | *Uriidu...min fadlik* |
| | اريد...من فضلك |

| – a can of shoe polish | *'ulba ma'juun li-talmii' al-ahdhiya* |
| | علبة معجون لتلميع الأحذية |

| – a pair of shoelaces | *zaw min ribaat al-hidhaa'* |
| | زوج من رباط الحذاء |

10.4 Cameras

I'd like a film for this camera, please	*Uriidu film lihaadhihi al-kamiira min fadlik* اريد فلم لهذه الكاميرا من فضلك
I'd like a cartridge, please	*Uriid khartuushat min fadlik* اريد خرطوشة من فضلك
– a one twenty-six cartridge	*khartuusha dhaat sit wa 'ishruun* خرطوشة ذات ست وعشرون
– a slide film	*film inzilaaqii* فيلم إنزلاقي
– a movie cassette, please	*shariit film min fadlik* شريط فيلم من فضلك
– a videotape	*shariit viidiyu* شريط فيديو
– color/black and white	*mulawwan/aswad wa abyad* ملون/اسود وابيض
– 12/24/36 exposures	*film dhuu 12/24/36 suura* فلم ذو 12/24/36 صورة
– ASA/DIN number	*raqm ay as ay/di aay an* رقم اي اس اي/دي آي أن

Problems

Could you load the film for me, please?	*Hal turakkib lii al-film min fadlik?* هل تركب لي الفلم من فضلك؟
Could you take the film out for me, please?	*Hal tukhrij lii al-film min fadlik?* هل تخرج لي الفلم من فضلك؟
Should I replace the batteries?	*Hal yajibu an ughayyira al-battaariyyaat?* هل يجب أن أغير البطاريات؟

Could you have a look at my camera, please?	*Hal tafhas al-kamira min fadlik?* هل تفحص الكامرا من فضلك؟
It's not working	*Innahaa laa ta'mal* إنها لا تعمل
The...is broken	*Al-...maksuur* ال...مكسور
The film's jammed	*Al-film mahshuur* الفلم محشور
The film's broken	*Al-film maksuur* الفلم مكسور
The flash isn't working	*Ad-daw' (al-flash) laa ya'mal* الضوء (الفلاش) لا يعمل

Processing and prints

I'd like to have this film developed and printed, please	*Min fadlik uriidu an atba'a haadha al-film* من فضلك اريد ان اطبع هذا الفلم
I'd like...prints from each negative	*Uriidu ...min kulli suura* اريد...من كل صورة
– glossy/matte	*laami'/naa'im* لامع/ناعم
– 6 x 9	*sitta fii tis'a* ستة في تسعة
I'd like to order reprints of these photos	*Uridu i'aadat tab' haadhihi as-suwar* اريد اعادة طبع هذه الصور
I'd like to have this photo enlarged	*Uriidu takbiir haadhihi as-suura* اريد تكبير هذه الصورة
How much is processing?	*Kam si'r at-tahmid?* كم سعر التحميض؟

How much for printing?	**Kam si'r at-tibaa'a?**
	كم سعر الطباعة؟
When will they be ready?	**Mataa takuun jaahiza?**
	متى تكون جاهزة؟

10.5 At the hairdresser

Do I have to make an appointment?	**Hal mina ad-daruurii an uhaddida maw'idan?**
	هل من الضروري أن أحدد موعدا؟
Can I come in right now?	**Hal astatii'u an adkhula al'aan?**
	هل استطيع ان ادخل الان؟
How long will I have to wait?	**Hal antaziru tawiilan?**
	هل انتظر طويلا؟
I'd like a shampoo/haircut	**Uriidu shaambuu/qassat sha'r**
	اريد شامبو/قصة شعر
I'd like a shampoo for oily/dry hair, please	**Min fadlik uriidu shaambuu lisha'r zaytii/jaaf**
	من فضلك اريد شامبو لشعر زيتي/جاف
I'd like an anti-dandruff shampoo	**Uriidu shaambuu did al-qishra**
	اريد شامبو ضد القشرة
I'd like a color-rinse shampoo, please	**Uriidu sibghat shaambuu mulawwin min fadlik**
	اريد صبغة شامبو ملون من فضلك
I'd like a shampoo with conditioner, please	**Uriidu shaambuu ma'a mulattif sha'r min fadlik**
	اريد شامبو مع ملطف شعر من فضلك
I'd like highlights, please	**Uriidu sabgha atraaf ash-sha'r min fadlik**
	اريد صبغ أطراف الشعر من فضلك

Do you have a color chart, please?	*Hal ladayka khariita al-alwaan min fadlik?* هل لديك خريطة الألوان، من فضلك؟
I'd like to keep the same color	*Uriid an uhaafiza 'alaa nafs al-lawn* اريد ان احافظ على نفس اللون
I'd like it darker/lighter	*Uriidu lawnan aghmaq/aftah* اريد لونا أغمق/أفتح
I'd like/I don't want hairspray	*Uriidu/laa uriidu rashaash sha'r* أريد/لا أريد رشاش شعر
– gel	*jall* جل
– lotion	*mustahdar* مستحضر
Not too short at the back	*Laysa qasiiran min al-khalf* ليس قصيرا من الخلف
Not too long	*Laysa tawiilan jiddan* ليس طويلا جدا
I'd like it curly/not too curly	*Uriiduhu muja'-'adan/laysa muja'-'adan* أريده مجعدا/ليس مجعدا
It needs a little/a lot taken off	*Yahtaaj an aqussa minhu qaliilan/kathiiran* يحتاج ان اقص منه قليلا/كثيرا
I'd like a completely different style/ a different/cut	*Uriidu tasriiha mukhtalifa tamaaman qassatan mukhtalifatan* أريد تسريحة مختلفة تماما/قصة مختلفة
I'd like it the same as in this photo	*Uriiduhu kamaa fii haadhihi as-suura* أريده كما في هذه الصورة
– as that woman's	*mithla tilka as-sayyida* مثل تلك السيدة

كيف تريد أن أقصه لك؟	How do you want it cut?
أية تسريحة تريد؟	What style do you have in mind?
أي لون تريد؟	What color do you want it?
هل درجة الحرارة مناسبة لك؟	Is the temperature all right for you?
هل ترغب في مطالعة بعض الصحف؟	Would you like something to read?
هل تريد مشروبا؟	Would you like a drink?
هل هذا ما أردت؟	Is this what you had in mind?

Could you turn the drier up/down a bit?	**hal yumkin an tukhaffifa/tuqawwiya al-mujaffif qaliilan?** هل يمكن ان تخفف/تقوي المجفف قليلا؟
I'd like a facial	**uriidu tadliik al-wajh** اريد تدليك الوجه
– a manicure	**sabgh azaafir al-yad** صبغ أظافر اليد
– a massage	**tadliik** تدليك
Could you give me a trim, please?	**hal tukhaffif lii sha'rii min fadlik?** هل تخفف لي شعري من فضلك؟
I'd like a shave, please	**Uriid an ahliqa lihyatii min fadlik** أريد أن أحلق لحيتي من فضلك
I'd like a wet shave, please	**Uriidu hilaaqat lihya muballala min fadlika** أريد حلاقة لحية مبللة من فضلك

11 Tourist Activities

11. Tourist Activities

11.1 Places of interest

● There are three main categories of tourist office: regional, provincial, and local. Regional offices are mainly concerned with planning and budgeting etc. Provincial offices usually have information on regions and towns. Tourist offices are generally open Saturday to Thursday 8.30 a.m. to 12.30 p.m. and 3.00 p.m. to 6.30 p.m.

Where's the Tourist Information, please?	*Law samahta, ayna maktabu al-ist'laamaat as-siyaahiya?* أين مكتب الاستعلامات السياحية؟
Do you have a city map?	*Hal ladayka khaaritat al-madiina?* هل لديك خارطة المدينة؟
Where is the museum?	*Ayna al-mathaf?* اين المتحف؟
Where can I find a church?	*Ayna yumkin an ajida kaniisa?* أين يمكن أن أجد كنيسة؟
Could you give me some information about...?	*Hal yumkin an tuzawwidanii bima'luumat 'an...?* هل يمكن ان تزودني بمعلومات عن...؟
How much is this?	*Maa si'r hadhaa?* ما سعر هذا؟
What are the main places of interest?	*Maa hiya al-mawaaqi' al-muhimma?* ماهي المواقع المهمة؟
Could you point them out on the map?	*Hal yumkin an tushira ilayhaa 'alaa al-khaarita min fadlik?* هل يمكن ان تشير اليها على الخارطة من فضلك؟
Sharm el-Sheikh is the City of Peace	*Sharm shI-Sheikh Madinat is-salam* شرم الشيخ مدينة السلام

The Burj Khalifa is the tallest building in the world
Burju Khalifa atwalu burj tii al-'aalam
برج خليفة أطول برج في العالم

Where is the Karnak Temple?
Ayna ma'bad al-karnak
أين معبد الكرنك؟

What do you recommend?
Bi-maadhaa tansah?
بم تنصح؟

We'll be here for a few hours
Sanabqaa hunaa li-bid'at saa'aat
سنبقى هنا لبضعة ساعات

We'll be here for a day
Sanabqaa hunaa li-yawmin waahid
سنبقى هنا ليوم واحد

We'll be here for a week
Sanabqaa hunaa li-muddat usbuu'
سنبقى هنا لمدة اسبوع

We're interested in...
Nahnu muhtammun bi...
نحن مهتمون ب...

قلعة
qal'aa
castle

مكتبة الإسكندرية
Maktabit al-Iskindiriya
the Library of Alexandria

الأهرام
Al-Ahraam
pyramids

معبد
ma'bad
temple

مدينة البتراء
Madinat al-patraa'
Petra city

القدس
Al-quds
Jerusalem

مدينة الأقصر
Al 'Uqsur
Luxor city

الهرم الأكبر
Al-Haram Al-Akbar
The Great Pyramid

بيت لحم
Bayt lahm
Bethlehem

مدينة أسوان
Aswan
Aswan city

المسرح الروماني
al-masrah ar-rumany
Roman theater

أبو الهول
Abou el-haul
Sphinx

غطس
ghats
diving

شعب مرجانية
shu'ab murjaniya
coral reef

I can't swim	*Anaa laa astaṯii' as-sibaaḥa* أنا لا أستطيع السباحة
I need swim fins	*Aḥtaaju za'aanif* أحتاج زعانف
Is there a scenic walk around the city?	*Hal hunaaka ṯariiqa tanazzuh ḥawla al-madiina?* هل هناك طريق تنزه حول المدينة؟
How long does it take?	*Kam tastaghriq?* كم تستغرق؟
Where does it start/end?	*Ayna tabda'/tantahii?* اين تبدأ/تنتهي؟
Are there any boat trips?	*Hal hunaaka ayyat raḥalaat baḥriyya?* هل هناك اية رحلات بحرية؟
Where can we board?	*Min ayna naṣ'ad ilaa al-markab?* من أين نصعد الى المركب؟
Are there any bus tours?	*Hal hunaaka ayyat raḥalaat bil-baaṣ?* هل هناك اية رحلات بالباص؟
Where do we get on?	*Min ayna narkab?* من أين نركب؟
Is there a guide who speaks English?	*Hal yuujad daliil siyaaḥii yatakallam al-inkiliiziyya?* هل يوجد دليل سياحي يتكلم الانكيزية؟
What trips can we take around the area?	*Ayyat raḥalaat yumkin an naquum bihaa ḥawla haadhihi al-minṯaqa?* اية رحلات يمكن ان نقوم بها حول هذه المنطقة؟
Are there any excursions?	*Hal hunaaka ayyat raḥalaat?* هل هناك اية رحلات؟
Where do they go?	*Ilaa ayna yadhhabuun?* إلى اين يذهبون؟

How long is the excursion?	*Kam sataduum ar-rihla?*
	كم ستدوم الرحلة؟
How long do we stay in...?	*Kam sanabqaa fii...?*
	كم سنبقى في...؟
Are there any guided tours?	*Hal hunaaka ayyat rahalaat yaquuduhaa daliil?*
	هل هناك اية رحلات يقودها دليل؟
How much free time will we have there?	*Kam sanabqaa hunaaka?*
	كم سنبقى هناك؟
Can we hire a guide?	*Hal yumkin an nasta'iina bi-daliil?*
	هل يمكن ان نستعين بدليل؟
We want to have a walk around/to go on foot	*Nuriidu an natamashaa fii al-mintaqa/ nuriidu an namshiya 'alaa al-aqdaam*
	نريد ان نتمشى في المنطقة/نريد ان نمشي على الأقدام
What time does...open/ close?	*Mataa yaftah/yughliq al...?*
	متى يفتح/يغلق ال...؟
What days are...open/ closed?	*Ay yawm yaftah/yughliq al...?*
	أي يوم يفتح/يغلق ال...؟
What's the admission price?	*Maa huwa rasm ad-dukhuul?*
	ما هو رسم الدخول؟
Is there a group discount?	*Hal hunaaka takhfiid lil-majmuu'aat?*
	هل هناك تخفيض للمجموعات؟
Is there a child discount?	*Hal hunaaka takhfiid lil-atfaal?*
	هل هناك تخفيض للاطفال؟
Is there a discount for senior citizens?	*Hal hunaaka takhfiid lil-musiniin?*
	هل هناك تخفيض للمسنين؟
Can I take (flash) photos/ can I film here?	*Hal astatii'u an aakhudha suwaran/ hal yumkin an usawwira hunaa?*
	هل استطيع ان آخذ صورا/هل يمكن ان اصور هنا؟

Do you have any postcards of...?	*Hal ladayka ayyat biṯaaqaat bariidiyya...?* هل لديك اية بطاقات بريدية لـ...؟
Do you have an English...?	*Hal ladayka...bil-lugha al-inkiliiziyya?* هل لديك...باللغة الانكليزية؟
– catalogue	*kataaluugh* كتالوغ
– program	*barnaamaj* برنامج
– brochure	*kurraasat namaadhij* كراسة نماذج

11.2 Going out

● Going out for artistic and cultural events depends very much on the specific city and country you are visiting. Generally speaking, most of the festivals, cultural events and concerts are organized during summer.

Do you have this week's/ month's entertainment guide?	*Hal ladayka daliil al-baraamij at-tarfiihiya lihaadhihi al-layla/ lihaadha ash-shahr?* هل لديك دليل البرامج الترفيهية لهذة الليلة/لهذا الشهر؟
What's on tonight?	*Maadhaa yuujad haadhihi al-layla?* ماذا يوجد هذه الليلة؟
We want to go to...	*Nuriidu an nadhhaba ilaa...* نريد ان نذهب الى...؟
What's playing at the cinema?	*Ay film yubath fii as-siinimaa?* أي فيلم يبث في السينما؟
What sort of film is that?	*Ay naw'in min al-aflaam haadha?* اي نوع من الافلام هذا؟

– suitable for everyone

yunaasib al-jamii'

يناسب الجميع

– not suitable for people under 12/under 16

laa yunaasib al-ashkhaas duuna sin ath-thaaniya 'ashara/as-saadisa 'ashara

لا يناسب الأشخاص دون سن الثانية عشرة/السادسة عشرة

– original version

an-nuskha al-asliyya

النسخة الاصلية

– subtitled

mu'anwan

معنون

– dubbed

mudablaj

مدبلج

Is it a continuous showing?

Hal haadhaa 'ard mustamir?

هل هذا عرض مستمر؟

What's on at...?

Maadhaa yuqaddam fii...?

ماذا يقدم في...؟

– the theater

al-masrah

المسرح

– the opera

al-uubiraa

الاوبرا

What's happening in the concert hall?

Maa huwa barnaamaj qaa'at al-muusiiqa?

ما هو برنامج قاعة الموسيقي؟

Where can I find a good disco around here?

Ayna yumkin an ajidaa diisku jayyid hunaa?

اين يمكن ان اجد ديسكو جيد هنا؟

Is it members only?

Hal haadhaa khaas bil-a'daa' al-muntasibiin faqat?

هل هذا خاص بالأعضاء المنتسبين فقط؟

Where can I find a good nightclub around here?	*Ayna yumkin an ajidaa naadii laylii jayyid hunaa?* اين يمكن ان اجد نادي ليلي جيد هنا؟
Is it evening wear only?	*Hal yajibu an artadiya libaasan khaasan bil-hafalaat al-masaa'iyya?* هل يجب أن أرتدي لباسا خاصا بالحفلات المسائية؟
Should I (we) dress up?	*Hal yajibu an albasa (nalbasa) libaasan rasmiyyan?* هل يجب اب البس (نلبس) لباسا رسميا؟
What time does the show start?	*Mataa yabda'u al-'ard?* متى يبدأ العرض؟
When's the next soccer match?	*Maa maw'id mubaaraat kurat al-qadam al-qaadima?* ما موعد مباراة كرة القدم القادمة؟
Who's playing?	*Man alladhii yal'ab?* من الذي يلعب؟
I'd like an escort for tonight	*Uriidu muraafiqan li-haadhihi al-layla* اريد مرافقا لهذه الليلة

11.3 Booking tickets

Could you reserve some tickets for us?	*Hal yumkin an tahjiza lanaa ba'd at-tadhaakir min fadlik?* هل يمكن ان تحجز لنا بعض التذاكر من فضلك؟
We'd like to book...seats/ a table for...	*Nuriidu an nahjiza...maqaa'id/ taawila li...* نريد ان نحجز...مقاعد/طاولة ل...؟
– seats in the circle	*maqaa'id fii ad-daa'ira* مقاعد في الدائرة

– a box for...	*ruknan li...* ...ركنا ل...
– seats in the orchestra in the main section	*maqaa'id fii al-urkistraa fii al-qism ar-ra'iisii* مقاعد في الاركسترا في القسم الرئيسي
– front row seats/a table for...at the front	*maqaa'id fii as-saf al-amaamii/ taawila li...fii al-amaam* مقاعد في الصف الامامي/طاولة ل... في الامام
– seats in the middle/a table in the middle	*maqaa'id fii al-wasat/taawila fii al-wasat* مقاعد في الوسط/طاولة في الوسط
– back row seats/a table at the back	*maqaa'id fii as-saf al-khalfii/taawila fii as-saf al-khalfi* مقاعد في الصف الخلفي/طاولة في الخلف
Could I reserve...seats for the...o'clock performance?	*Hal yumkin an ahjiza...maqaa'id li'ard as-saa'a...?* هل يمكن ان احجز...مقاعد لعرض الساعة...؟
Are there any seats left for tonight?	*Hal tuujad ayyat tadhaakir mutabaqiya lihaadhihi al-layla?* هل توجد اية تذاكر متبقية لهذه الليلة؟
How much is a ticket?	*Kam si'r at-tadhkira?* كم سعر التذكرة؟
When can I pick up the tickets?	*Mataa yumkin an astalima at-tadhaakir?* متى يمكن ان استلم التذاكر؟
I've got a reservation	*Ladayya hajz* لدي حجز
My name's...	*Ismii...* ...اسمي

تريد ان تحجز لأي عرض؟	Which performance do you want to reserve for?
اين تريد ان تجلس؟	Where would you like to sit?
بيع كل شيء	Everything's sold out
غرفة للوقوف فقط	It's standing room only
لدينا مقاعد دائرية فقط	We've only got circle seats left
لدينا مقاعد دائرية عليا فقط	We've only got upper circle (way upstairs) seats left
لدينا مقاعد للفرقة الموسيقية فقط	We've only got orchestra seats left
هناك مقاعد في الصف الامامي	We've only got front row seats left
هناك مقاعد في المؤخرة	We've only got seats left at the back
كم مقعدا تريد؟	How many seats would you like?
يجب أن تستلم التذاكر قبل الساعة ...	You'll have to pick up the tickets before...o'clock
التذاكر من فضلك	Tickets, please
هذا مقعدك	This is your seat
أنت في المقعد الخطأ	You are in the wrong seat

12 Sports Activities

12. Sports Activities

12.1 Sporting questions

Where can we...around here?	*Ayna yumkin an...hunaa?* اين يمكن ان...هنا ؟
Can we hire a...?	*Hal yumkinuni an asta'jira...?* هل يمكنني ان استأجر...؟
Can we take lessons?	*Hal yumkin an natalaqaa duruusan?* هل يمكن ان نتلقى دروسا ؟
For beginners/ intermediates	*Lil-mubtadi'iin/al-mutawassitiin* للمبتدئين/للمتوسطين
How large are the groups?	*Maa hajm al-majmuu'aat?* ما حجم للمجموعات؟
What languages are the classes in?	*Bi-ayyati lugha tu'taa ad-duruus?* بأية لغة تعطى الدروس؟
How much is that per hour/per day?	*Kam al-ujra fii as-saa'a/al-yawm?* كم الاجرة في الساعة/اليوم؟
How much is each one?	*Kam si'r al-waahid?* كم سعر الواحد؟
Do you need a permit for that?	*Hal tahtaaj ilaa rukhsa li-haadhaa?* هل تحتاج الى رخصة لهذا ؟
Where can I get the permit?	*Min ayna yumkin al-husuul 'alaa rukhsa?* من اين يمكن الحصول على رخصة؟

12.2 By the waterfront

Is it far to walk to the sea?	*Hal yumkin an adhhaba ilaa al-bahri mashyan?* هل يمكن أن أذهب الى البحر مشيا؟
Is there a...around here?	*Hal yuujad...huna?* هل يوجد...هنا؟
– a swimming pool	*masbah* مسبح
– a sandy beach	*shaati' ramlii* شاطئ رملي
– a nudist beach	*shaati' lil-'uraat* شاطئ للعراة
– a mooring place/dock	*marsaa/rasiif* رصيف/مرسى
Are there any rocks here?	*Hal tuujad ay sukhuur hunaa?* هل توجد أي صخور هنا؟
When's high/low tide?	*Mataa yakuun a'laa/aqal mustawaa lil-mad?* متى يكون أعلى/اقل مستوى للمد؟
What's the water temperature?	*Maa hiya darajat haraarat al-maa'?* ما هي درجة حرارة الماء؟
Is it very deep here?	*Hal haadha 'amiiq jiddan?* هل هذا عميق جدا؟
Is it safe for children to swim here?	*Hal yumkin lil-atfaal an yasbahuu hunaa bi-amaan?* هل يمكن للاطفال ان يسبحوا هنا بأمان؟
Are there any currents?	*Hal tuujad tayyaaraat?* هل توجد تيارات؟

Are there any rapids along this river?	*Hal tuujad ayyat munhadaraat aw shallaalaat fii haadhaa an-nahr?* هل توجد اية منحدرات او شلالات في هذا النهر؟
What does that flag/buoy mean?	*Maadhaa ya'nii dhaalika al-'alam/al-'awwaama?* ماذا يعني ذلك العلم/العوامة؟
Is there a lifeguard on duty?	*Hal yuujad rajul inqaadh?* هل يوجد رجل انقاذ؟
Are dogs allowed here?	*Hal masmuuh bil-kilaab hunaa?* هل مسموح بالكلاب هنا؟
Is camping on the beach allowed?	*Hal yusmah bi-nasbi al-khiyaam fii haadhaa ash-shaati'?* هل يسمح بنصب الخيام في هذا الشاطيء؟
Can we light a fire?	*Hal yumkin an nush'ila an-naar?* هل يمكن ان نشعل النار؟

مياه الصيد
miyaah as-sayd
Fishing waters

منوع السباحة
mamnuu' as-sibaaha
No swimming

برخصة فقط
birukhsa faqat
Permits only

خطر
khatar
Danger

ممنوع التزلج الشراعي
mamnuu' at-tazalluj ash-shiraa'ii
No surfing

ممنوع الصيد
mamnuu' as-sayd
No fishing

13 Health Matters

13. Health Matters

13.1 Calling a doctor

● If you become ill or need emergency treatment, it is best to go to Casualty (*istijalii*) at your nearest hospital.

Could you call a doctor quickly, please?	*Hal yumkin an tattaṣil biṭabiib bisur'a min faḍlik?* هل يمكن ان تتصل بطبيب بسرعة من فضلك؟
When does the doctor have office hours?	*Maa hiya saa'aat 'amal aṭ-ṭabiib?* ماهي ساعات عمل الطبيب؟
When can the doctor come?	*Mataa ya'tii aṭ-ṭabiib?* متى يأتي الطبيب؟
Could I make an appointment to see the doctor?	*Hal yumkin an uḥaddida maw'idan liziyaarat aṭ-ṭabiib?* هل يمكن ان أحدد موعدا لزيارة الطبيب؟
I've got an appointment to see the doctor at...o'clock	*Ladayya maw'id ma'a aṭ-ṭabiib 'alaa sa-saa'a...* لدي موعد مع الطبيب على الساعة...
Which doctor/pharmacy is on night/ weekend duty?	*Ay ṭabiib/ṣaydaliyya maftuuḥ laylan/khilaal 'uṭlat nihaayat al-usbuu'?* أي طبيب/صيدلية مفتوح ليلا/خلال عطلة نهاية الاسبوع؟

13.2 What's wrong?

I don't feel well	*Ash'uru bi-'alam* اشعر بالم
I'm dizzy	*Ash'uru bi-duwaar* اشعر بدوار

– ill	*mariid*
	مريض
I feel sick (nauseous)	*Ash'uru bi-raghba fii at-taqayyu'*
	اشعر برغبة في التقيؤ
I've got a cold	*'indii zukaam*
	عندي زكام
It hurts here	*Al-alam hunaa*
	الالم هنا
I've been sick (vomited)	*Kuntu ataqayya'*
	كنت اتقيأ
I've got...	*'indii/ash'uru bi*
	أشعر ب.. /عندي
I'm running a temperature of...degrees	*Haraaratii hiya...darajaat*
	حرارتي هي...درجات
I've been...	*Kuntu...*
	...كنت
– stung by a wasp	*ladaghatnii nahlaa*
	لدغتني نحلة
– stung by an insect	*ladaghatnii hashara*
	لدغتني حشرة
– bitten by a dog	*'addanii kalb*
	عضني كلب
– stung by a jellyfish	*ladaghanii qandiil al-bahr*
	لدغتني قنديل البحر
– bitten by a snake	*ladaghatnii hayya*
	لدغتني حية
– bitten by an animal	*'addanii hayawaan*
	عضني حيوان

English	Arabic (transliteration)
I've cut myself	*Jarahtu nafsii* جرحت نفسي
I've burned myself	*Haraqtu nafsii* حرقت نفسي
I've grazed/scratched myself	*Khadashtu/hakaktu nafsii* خدشت/حككت نفسي
I've had a fall	*Waqa'tu 'alaa al-ard* وقعت على الارض
I've sprained my ankle	*Iltawaa kahilii/ka'ibii* التوى كاحلي/كعبي
I'd like the morning-after pill	*Ufadilu hubuub mani' al-haml as-sabaahiya* افضل حبوب منع الحمل الصباحية

13.3 The consultation

ما المشكلة؟	What seems to be the problem?
منذ متى تشكو من هذا	How long have you had these complaints?
هل حصلت لك هذه المشكلة من قبل؟	Have you had this trouble before?
هل تعرف درجة حرارتك؟ ماهي؟	Do you have a temperature? What is it?
اخلع (انزع) ثيابك من فضلك	Get undressed, please
انزع الى حد الخصر من فضلك	Strip to the waist, please
يمكن ان تنزع ثيابك هناك	You can undress there

اكشف عن ذراعك الايمان/ الايسر من فضلك	Roll up your left/right sleeve, please
استلق هنا من فضلك	Lie down here, please
هل هذا يؤلمك؟	Does this hurt?
خذ نفسا عميقا	Breathe deeply
افتح فمك	Open your mouth

Patients' medical history

I'm a diabetic
'Indii as-sukkarii
عندي السكري

I have a heart condition
U'aanii min marad al-qalb
اعاني من مرض القلب

I'm asthmatic
U'aanii min ar-rabuu
اعاني من الربو

I'm allergic to...
Ladayya hassaasiyya didda...
لدي حساسية ضد...

I'm...months pregnant
Anaa haamil fii ash-shahr...
انا حامل في الشهر...

I'm on a diet
Ladayya nizaam ghidhaa'ii
لدي نظام غذائي

I'm on medication/ the pill
Utaabi'u 'ilaajan/atanaawalu hubuuban
أتابع علاجا/أتناول حبوباً

I've had a heart attack once before
Ta'arradtu li'azma qalbiyya marratan waahida fii as-sabiq
تعرضت لازمة قلبية مرة واحدة في السابق

I've had an operation on my...
Ujriyat 'alayya 'amaliyya jirahiyya fii...
أجريت على عملية جراحية في...

I've been ill recently	*Asbahtu mariidan mundhu waqtin qasiirin* أصبحت مريضا منذ وقت قصير
I've got a stomach ulcer	*'Indii qurh fii al-ma'ida* عندي قرح في المعدة
I've got my period	*Anaa fii ad-dawra ash-shahriyya* انا في الدورة الشهرية

هل لديك اية حساسية؟	Do you have any allergies?
هل تتابع اي علاج حاليا ؟	Are you on any medication?
هل لديك نظام غذائي ؟	Are you on a diet?
هل انت حامل؟	Are you pregnant?
هل سبق ان اخذت حقنة ضد الكزاز ؟	Have you had a tetanus injection?

The diagnosis

لا شيء خطر	It's nothing serious
...مكسور	Your...is broken
لديك...إلتواء في	You've got a sprained...
لديك...تمزق	You've got a torn...
لديك التهاب/بعض التورم	You've got an infection/some inflammation
لديك التهاب الزائدة	You've got appendicitis
لديك التهاب رئوي	You've got bronchitis
لديك مرض تناسلي	You've got a venereal disease
انت مصاب بالانفلونزا	You've got the flu

167

تعرضت لازمة قلبية	You've had a heart attack
لديك التهاب بكتيري/فيروسي	You've got a (viral/bacterial) infection
لديك التهاب رئوي حاد	You've got pneumonia
لديك التهاب/قرح في المعدة	You've got gastritis/an ulcer
لديك تمطط عضلي	You've pulled a muscle
لديك التهاب في المهبل	You've got a vaginal infection
أصبت بتسمم غذائي	You've got food poisoning
أصبت بضربة شمس	You've got sunstroke
لديك حساسية ضد...	You're allergic to...
انت حامل	You're pregnant
اريد تحليل دمك/بولك/برازك	I'd like to have your blood/urine/stools tested
هذا يحتاج الى تغريز	It needs stitches
احيلك الى طبيب اخصائي/ارسلك الى المستشفى	I'm referring you to a specialist/sending you to the hospital
انت تحتاج الى فحص اشعة أكس	You'll need some X-rays taken
هل يمكن ان تنتظر في قاعة الانتظار من فضلك؟	Could you wait in the waiting room, please?
انت تحتاج الى عملية جراحية	You'll need an operation

Is it contagious?	*Hal haadhaa marad mu'dii?* هل هذا مرض معدي؟
How long do I have to stay...?	*Kam yajib an abqaa...?* كم يجب ان ابقى...؟
– in bed	*fii al-firaash* في الفراش
– in the hospital	*fii al-mustashfaa* في المستشفى

Do I have to go on a special diet?	*Hal yajib an utaabi'a nizaaman ghidhaa'iian khaasan* هل يجب ان اتابع نظاما غذائيا خاصا؟
Am I allowed to travel?	*Hal masmuhun lii bis-safar?* هل مسموح لي بالسفر؟
Can I make another appointment?	*Hal yumkin an uhaddida maw'idan aakhar?* هل يمكن ان أحدد موعدا اخر؟
When do I have to come back?	*Maa huwa maw'id al-fahis al-qaadim?* ما هو موعد الفحص القادم؟
I'll come back tomorrow	*Sawfa aatii ghadan* سوف آتي غدا
How do I take this medicine?	*Kayfa aakhudhu haadhaa d-dawaa'?* كيف آخذ هذا الدواء؟

تعال غدا/خلال...ايام   Come back tomorrow/ in...days' time

Medications and prescriptions

How many pills/drops/ injections/spoonfuls/ tablets each time?	*Kam kabsuula/qatara/huqna/mil'aqa/ habba fii kul marra?* كم كبسولة/قطرة/حقنة/ملعقة/ حبة في كل مرة؟
How many times a day?	*Kam marra fii al-yawm?* كم مرة في اليوم؟
I've forgotten my medication.	*Nasiitu ad-dawaa'* نسيت الدواء
At home I take...	*Fii al-bayt aakhudhu...* في البيت آخذ...

| Could you write a prescription for me, please? | **Hal yumkin an taktuba lii waṣfa min faḍlik?** |
| | هل يمكن ان تكتب لي وصفة من فضلك؟ |

كتبت لك مضاد حيوي/ خليط/مهدي،/مسكن الالم	I'm prescribing antibiotics/a mixture/a tranquillizer/pain killers
عليك بالراحة	Have lots of rest
ابق في البيت	Stay indoors
لازم الفرابق	Stay in bed

كبسول
kabsuul
pills

حبوب
hubuub
tablets

أكمل الوصفة
akmil al-waṣfa
finish the prescription

ملعقة/ملعقة شاي
mal'aqat/mal'aqat shaay
spoonful/teaspoonful

حل (ذوب) في الماء
hil (dhawwib) fii al-maa'
dissolve in water

ابلع
ibla'
swallow (whole)

حقنات
huqnaat
injections

قطرات
qaṭraat
drops

كل...ساعات
kul...saa'aat
every...hours

مرهم
marham
ointment

خد
khud
take

لمدة...ايام
limuddat... ayyaam
for...days

قبل الوجبات
qabla al-wajbaat
before meals

هذا العلاج يؤثر على السياقة
haadha al-'ilaaj yu'athir 'laa as-siyaaqa
this medication impairs your driving

استعمال خار جي فقط
isti'maal khaarijii faqat
external use only

دلك
dalk
rub on

مرات في اليوم
...marraat fii al-yawm
...times a day

13.5 At the dentist

Do you know a good dentist?	*Hal ta'rif tabiib asnaan jayyid?* هل تعرف طبيب اسنان جيد؟
Could you make a dental appointment for me?	*Hal yumkin an tuhaddida lii maw'idan ma'a tabiib al-asnan?* هل يمكن ان تحدد لي موعدا مع طبيب اسنان؟
It's urgent	*Musta'jal* مستعجل
Can I come in today, please?	*Hal astatii' an aa-tiya al-yawm?* هل استطيع ان آتي اليوم؟
I have a terrible toothache	*U'aanii min alam shadiid fii al-asnaan* أعاني من الم شديد في الاسنان
My filling's come out	*Saqatat al-hashwa* سقطت الحشوة
Could you prescribe/give me a painkiller?	*Hal yumkin an tasifa lii/tu'tiyanii musakkin lil-alam?* هل يمكن أن تصف لي/تعطيني مسكن للالم؟
I've got a broken tooth	*Ladayya sinn maksuur* لدي سن مكسور
I've got a broken crown	*Ladayya kasr fii taaj as-sinn* لدي كسر في تاج السن
I'd like/I don't want a local anesthetic	*Uriidu/laa uriidu takhdiir mawdi'ii* اريد/لا اريد تخدير موضعي
Could you do a temporary repair?	*Hal yumkin an uslihahu mu'aqqatan?* هل يمكن ان تصلحة مؤقتا؟
I don't want this tooth pulled	*Laa uridu qal'a haadhaa as-sinn* لا اريد قلع هذا السن

My denture is broken	*Fakkii al-istinaa'ii maksur*
	فكي الاصطناعي مكسور
Can you fix it?	*Hal yumkin an tuslihahu?*
	هل يمكن ان تصلحه؟

اي سن يؤلمك؟	Which tooth hurts?
لديك صديد	You've got an abscess
يجب ان أفحص قناة جذر السن	I'll have to do a root canal
ساعطيك تخدير موضعي	I'm giving you a local anesthetic
يجب ان اقلع/احشي/ابرد هذا السن	I'll have to pull/fill/file this tooth
يجب ان أحفره	I'll have to drill it
افتح فمك من فضلك	Open wide, please
اغلق من فضلك	Close your mouth, please
اغسل من فضلك	Rinse, please
هل ما زال يؤلمك؟	Does it hurt still?

14 Emergencies

14. Emergencies

14.1 Asking for help

Help!	*An-najda!* النجدة
Fire!	*Hariiq/naar!* حريق / نار
Police!	*Yaa buuliis (shurta)!* يا بوليس (شرطة)
Quick/Hurry!	*'Ajjil/bisur'a!* عجل / بسرعه
Danger!	*Khatar!* خطر
Watch out!	*Ihdhar!* احذر
Stop!	*Qif!* قف
Be careful!/Go easy!	*Ihdhar (intabih)/tamahhal!* احذر (انتبه) / تمهل
Get your hands off me!	*Irfa' yadaka 'annii!* ارفع يدك عني
Let go!	*Utruknii!* اتركنى
Stop thief!	*Awqif al-lis!* اوقف اللص
Could you help me, please?	*Hal yumkin an tusaa'idanii min fadlik?* هل يمكن ان تساعدني من فضلك؟

Where's the nearest fire extinguisher?	*Ayna ajid aqrab qanninat itfaa' al-hariiq?* أين اجد اقرب قنينة اطفاء الحريق؟
Where's the police station/emergency exit/fire escape?	*Ayna markaz ash-shurta/makhraj at-tawaari'/mahrab al-hariiq?* أين مركز الشرطة/مخرج الطوارىء/ مهرب الحريق؟
Call the fire department!	*Utlub rijaal al-matafi'!* أطلب رجال المطافىء
Call the police!	*Utlub (ittasil bi) ash-shurta!* اطلب (اتصل ب) الشرطة
Call an ambulance!	*Utlub (ittasil bi) sayyaarat al-is'aaf!* اطلب (اتصل ب) سيارة الاسعاف
Where's the nearest phone?	*Ayna ajidu aqraba haatif?* اين اجد اقرب هاتف؟
Could I use your phone?	*Hal yumkin an astakhdima haatifaka* هل يمكن ان استخدم هاتفك؟
What's the emergency number?	*Maa huwa raqm haatif at-tawaari'?* ما هو رقم هاتف الطوارىء؟
What's the number for the police?	*Maa raqm haatif ash-shurta?* ما رقم هاتف الشرطة؟

14.2 Lost items

I've lost my wallet	*Faqadtu mihfazatii* فقدت محفظتي
I lost my...here yesterday	*Faqadtu...hunaa amsi* فقدت...هنا امس
I left my...here	*Taraktu...hunaa* تركت...هنا

Did you find my...?	*Hal wajadta...?* هل وجدت...؟
It was right here	*Kaanat hunaa* كانت هنا
It's very valuable	*Innahu thamiin jiddan* انه ثمين جدا
Where's the lost and found office?	*Ayna daa'irat al-bahthi 'an almafquudaat* اين دائرة البحث عن المفقودات؟

14.3 Accidents

There's been an accident	*Waqa'a haadith* وقع حادث
Someone's fallen into the water	*Saqata shakhsun fii l-maa'* سقط شخص في الماء
There's a fire	*Hunaaka hariiq* هناك حريق
Is anyone hurt?	*Hal ta'arrada ayya shakhsin lil-adhaa?* هل تعرض اي شخص للأذى؟
Nobody/someone has been injured	*Laa ahada/shakhsun maa juriha* لا أحد/شخص ماجرح
Someone's still trapped inside the car/train	*Maa zaala shakhsun maa mahbuusun daakhila as-sayyaara/al-qitaar* مازال شخص ما محبوس داخل السيارة/القطار
It's not too bad	*Al-haala laysat sayyi'a jiddan* الحالة ليست سيئة جدا
Don't worry	*Laa taqlaq* لا تقلق

Leave everything the way it is, please
Utruk kulla shay'in kamma huwa, min fadlik
اترك كل شيء كما هو من فضلك

I want to talk to the police first
Uriidu an atahaddatha ila ash-shurta awwalan
اريد ان اتحدث الى الشرطة اولا

I want to take a photo first
Uriidu an altaqita suuratan awwalan
اريد ان ألتقط صورة اولا

Here's my name and address
Haadhaa ismii wa 'unwaanii
هذا اسمي وعنواني

May I have your name and address?
Al-'ism wa al-'unwaan law samahta
الإسم و العنوان لو سمحت؟

Could I see your identity card/your insurance papers?
Min fadlik bitaaqatuka ash-shakhsiyya/ awraaq at-ta'miin?
من فضلك بطاقتك الشخصية/ اوراق التأمين؟

Will you act as a witness?
Hal yumkin an tadliya bi-shahaada?
هل يمكن ان تدلي بشهادة؟

I need this information for insurance purposes
Ahtaaju li-haadhihi al-ma'luumaat li- 'aghraad at-ta'miin
احتاج لهذه المعلومات لأغراض التأمين

Are you insured?
Hal anta mu'amman?
هل أنت مؤمن؟

Third party or all inclusive?
Ta'miin juz'ii am shaamil?
تأمين جزئي أم شامل؟

Could you sign here, please?
Hal yumkin an tuwaqqi'a hunaa min fadlika?
هل يمكن ان توقع هنا من فضلك؟

14.4 Theft

I've been robbed	*Ta'arradtu lis-sariqa* تعرضت للسرقة
My...has been stolen	*...suriqa minnii* ...سرق مني
My car's been broken into	*Sayyaratii khuli'at* سيارتي خلعت

14.5 Missing person

I've lost my child/ grandmother	*Faqadtu tiflii/jaddatii* فقدت طفلي/جدتي
Could you help me find him/her?	*Hal tusaa'idunii fii al-bahthi 'anhu/ 'anhaa?* هل تساعدني في البحث عنه/عنها؟
Have you seen a small child?	*Hal ra'ayta tifl saghiir?* هل رأيت طفلا صغيرا؟
She's/he's...years old	*'Umruhaa/'umruhu...sana* عمرها/عمره...سنة
He's/she's got...hair	*Sha'ruhu/sha'ruhaa...al-lawn* شعره/شعرها...اللون
– short/long	*tawiil/qasiir* طويل/قصير
– blond/red/brown/ black/gray	*ashqar/ahmar/bunnii/aswad/ramaadii* اشقر/احمر/بني/اسود/رمادي
– curly/straight/frizzy	*muja'ad/musbal/muja'ad* مجعد/مسبل/مجعد
– in a ponytail	*tasriihat dhayl al-hisaan* تسريحة ذيل الحصان

– in braids	**dafaa'ir** ضفائر
– in a bun	**tasriiha** تسريحة
He's/she's got blue/ brown/green eyes	**'Aynaah/'aynaahaa khadraawaan/ zarqaawaan/buniyyataan** عيناه/عيناها خضراوان/زرقاوان/بنيتان
He/she's wearing…	**Huwa yalbas/hiya talbas…** هو يلبس/هي تلبس...
– swimming trunks/ hiking boots	**tubbaan sibaha/hidhaa' tasalluq al-jibaal** تبان سباحة/حذاء تسلق الجبال
– with/without glasses	**laabis/biduun nazzaraat** لابس/بدون نظارات
– carrying/not carrying a bag	**yahmil/laa yahmil haqiiba** يحمل/لا يحمل حقيبة
He/She is short	**Huwa qasiir/hiya qasiira** هو قصير/هي قصيرة
This is a photo of him/her	**Haadhihi suuratuhu/suuratuhaa** هذه صورته/صورتها
He must be lost	**Innahu laa budda an yakuun mafquuda** إنه لابد أن يكون مفقودا
She must be lost	**Innahaa laa budda an takuun mafquuda** انها لا بد ان تكون مفقودة

14.6 The police

An arrest

I don't speak Arabic	**Anaa laa atakallamu al-'arabiyya** انا لا اتكلم العربية

وثائقك (اوراق) سيارتك من فضلك	Your (vehicle) documents, please
كنت تسوق بسرعة	You were speeding
لا يسمح لك بايقاف سيارتك هنا	You're not allowed to park here
لم تضع نقودا في عداد الموقف	You haven't put money in the parking meter
مصابيحك لا تعمل	Your lights aren't working
ستدفع مخالفة	You'll have to pay a fine
هل تريد ان تدفع الآن	Do you want to pay now?
يجب عليك ان تدفع الآن	You'll have to pay now

I didn't see the sign	**Lam ara al-'alaama** لم ار العلامة
I don't understand what it says	**Laa afahamu maa ta'niihi** لا أفهم ما تعنيه
I was only doing... kilometers an hour	**Kuntu asuuqu bisur'at...kiilumatr fii as-saa'a** كنت اسوق بسرعة...كيلومتر في الساعة
I'll have my car checked	**Uriidu an afhasa sayyaaratii** أريد ان افحص سيارتي
I was blinded by oncoming lights	**A'maa 'aynii daw' as-sayyaaraat al-muqaabila** أعمى عيني ضوء السيارات المقابلة

أين حصل هذا؟	Where did it happen?
ما المفقود؟	What's missing?
ماذا اخذ منك؟	What's been taken?

هل يمكن ان ارى بطاقتك الشخصية/ اية اثباتات شخصية؟	Could I see your identity card/ some identification?
متى حصل ذلك؟	What time did it happen?
هل يوجد اي شهود؟	Are there any witnesses?
وقع هنا لو سمحت	Sign here, please
هل تحتاج الى مترجم؟	Do you want an interpreter?

At the police station

I want to report a collision/ missing person/rape	*Uriidu an ukhbira 'an haadith tasaadum /shakhs mafquud/ightisaab* اريد ان اخبر عن حادث تصادم/ شخص مفقود/اغتصاب
Could you make a statement, please?	*Hal yumkin an taktuba tasriihan min fadlik?* هل يمكن ان تكتب تصريحا من فضلك؟
Could I have a copy for the insurance?	*Hal yumkin an ahsula 'alaa nuskha li-sharikat at-ta'miin?* هل يمكن ان احصل على نسخة لشركة التأمين؟
I've lost everything	*Faqadtu kulla shay'* فقدت كل شيء
I've no money left, I'm desperate	*Lam tabqa ladayya ayyat nuquud anaa fii wad'in harijin* لم تبق لدي اية نقود انا في وضع حرج
Could you lend me a little money?	*Hal yumkin an tuqridanii ba'da l-maal?* هل يمكن ان تقرضني بعض المال؟
I'd like an interpreter	*Ahtaaju ilaa mutarjim* أحتاج إلى مترجم

I'm innocent	*Anaa barii'* أنا بريء
I don't know anything about it	*Laa a'rifu ay <u>sh</u>ay' 'anhu/'anhaa* لا أعرف اي شيء عنه/عنها
I want to speak to someone from the American embassy	*Uriidu an ata<u>h</u>adda<u>th</u>a ilaa <u>sh</u>akhsin min as-safaara al-amariikiyya* اريد ان اتحدث الى شخص من السفارة الامريكية
I want a lawyer who speaks...	*Uriidu mu<u>h</u>aamiyan yatakallamu al-lu<u>gh</u>a...* اريد محاميا يتكلم اللغة...

15 **Politics**

15. Politics

15.1 Government

مرشح للرئاسة *murashah lilr'iaasa* presidential candidate	ملك *malik* king	الجيش *al-jaish* army
رئيس الدولة *Ra'iis el-dawla* President of the State	أمير *amir* prince	الشرطة *al-shorta* the police
الرئيس السابق *ar-ra'iis al sabiq* former president	جمهورية *jumhuriya* republic	حكم عسكري *hukm 'askarii* military rule
نائب الرئيس *naa'ib ar-ra'iis* vice-president	مملكة *mamlaka* kingdom	حكم مدني *hukm madanii* civilian rule
رئيس الوزراء *ra'iis al-wuzaraa'* prime minister	وزير *waziir* minister	حكم ديني *hukm diinii* religious rule
القوات المسلحة *al-quwaat al-musallaha* military forces	برلمان *barlamaan* parliament	انتخابات *entihkaabaat* elections

Who is the president of Algeria?	*Man ra'iis al- jazaa'ir?* من رئيس الجزائر؟
Who is the king of Saudi Arabia?	*Man malik as-sa'udiya?* من ملك السعودية؟

15.2 Political trends

● Most Arabic countries have a constitution and different political parties, but some Arabic countries do not have a constitution and do not allow any political party.

Are you Socialist or Liberal?

Hal anta ishteraky am libraly?
هل أنت اشتراكي أم ليبرالي؟

سياسة *siyaasa* policy	شيوعية *shiyu'iya* communism	ليبرالية *libraliya* liberalism
سياسي *siyaasy* political	شيوعي *shiyu'i* communist	ليبرالي *libraly* liberal
ديمقراطية *dimoqratiya* democracy	إسلامي *Islamy* Islamist	سلفي *salafy* retroactive
ديمقراطي *dimoqrati* democratic	الأخوان المسلمون *Al-ikhwan al-muslemuun* Muslim brotherhood	حزب *hizb* party
ديكتاتورية *diktaturiya* dictatorship	الجماعة الإسلامية *al-jama'a al-islamiya* Islamist groups	حزب الأغلبية *hizb al-aghlabiya* the majority party
ديكتاتور *diktatur* dictator	منظمات المجتمع المدني *munazzamaat al-mujtam'* *al-madanii* civil society organizations	أقلية *aqalliya* minority
اشتراكية *ishterakiya* socialism	جامعة الدول العربية *Jami'at ad-duwal al-'arabiya* The Arab League	حقوق الإنسان *huquuq al-insaan* human rights
اشتراكي *ishteraky* socialist	الأمم المتحدة *Al-umam al-muttahida* United Nations	حقوق المرأة *huquuq al-mar'a* women's rights

15.3 Arab Spring

● The Arab Spring is a revolutionary wave of demonstrations and protests in the Arab world that began on 18 December 2010. Rulers have been forced from power in Tunisia, Egypt, Libya, Yemen and elsewhere.

ثورة	مظاهرة	حرية	فساد
thaura	*muzahara*	*hurriya*	*fasaad*
revolution	demonstration	freedom	corruption
اعتراض	متظاهرون	مساواة	
i'tiraad	*mutazahiruun*	*musaawaa*	
protest	demonstrators	equality	

15.4 Arab-Israeli conflict

● The Arab-Israeli conflict involves political tensions and open hostilities between the Arab peoples and the Jewish community of the Middle East. The roots of the modern Arab-Israeli conflict lie in the rise of Zionism and Arab nationalism towards the end of the nineteenth century.

منظمة التحرير الفلسطينية	اللاجئين	معاهدة
Munazzamat at-tahriir al-falastiiniya	*al-laji'iin*	*mu'aahada*
Palestine Liberation Organization	refugees	treaty
قضية فلسطين	حق العودة	تطبيع
Qadiyat falastiin	*Haqu al-'auda*	*tatbii'*
Palestinian case	right of return	normalization
	حرب	مفاوضات
	harb	*mufaawadaat*
	war	negotiation

16

Religion

16. Religion

Religion

● The majority of Arab people are Muslim, but there are Christian and Jewish minorities.

الإسلام	المسيحية	مسيحي	كاثوليكي	نبي
Al-islam	*Al-masiihiya*	*Masiihii*	*Kathuliki*	*Nabiyu*
Islam	Christianity	Christian	Catholic	Prophet
مسلم	اليهودية	كنيسة	الله	رسول
Muslim	*Al-yahuudiya*	*kaniisa*	*Allah*	*Rasuul*
Muslim	Judaism	church	The God	Messenger
سني	أرثوذكسي	يهودي	إله	مذهب
Sunnii	*Arthudhuksi*	*Yahuudii*	*Ilaah*	*madh'hab*
Sunni	Orthodox	Jewish	God	doctrine
شيعي	بروتستانت	معبد	رب	حج
Shii'ii	*Prutestaant*	*ma'bad*	*Rab*	*Hajju*
Shia	Protestant	temple	Lord	pilgrimage
مسجد	ملحد	دين	صلاة	صوم
masjid	*mulhid*	*diin*	*salaa*	*saum*
mosque	atheist	religion	prayer	fasting
حائط المبكى				
haa'itu al-mabkaa				
Wailing Wall				

Kaaba is the House of God	*Al-ka'ba baitu allah* الكعبة بيت الله
Are you Muslim or Christian?	*Hal anta mulim am masiihii?* هل أنت مسلم أم مسيحي؟

I am Christian	*Anaa masii__hii__*
	أنا مسيحي
Do you believe in God?	*Hal tu'min billah?*
	هل تؤمن بالله؟
What is your religion?	*Maa diinuk?*
	ما دينك؟
I do not have a religion	*Laa deen lii*
	لا دين لي

17

English–
Arabic
Word List

English-Arabic Word List   191-224

17. English-Arabic Word List

● The following word list is meant to supplement the chapters in this book. Some of the words not on this list can be found elsewhere in this book. Food items can be found in Sections 4.7 and 4.8, the parts of car from pages 80-81, the parts of a bicycle on pages 86-87 and camping/backpacking equipment on pages 114-115.

A

about حوالي/تقريبا *hawaalay/ taqriiban*

above أعلى/فوق *fawq/a'laa*

abroad في خارج البلاد *fii khaarij al-bilaad*

accident حادث *haadith*

adaptor وصلة *wasla*

address عنوان *'unwaan*

admission دخول *dukhuul*

admission price رسم الدخول *rasm ad-ukhuul*

adult بالغ، كهل *baaligh, kahl*

advice نصيحة *nasiiha*

airplane طائرة *taa'ira*

after بعد *ba'd*

afternoon مساء *massa'*

aftershave كولونيا *kulunya*

again مرة اخرى *marra ukhraa*

against ضد/مقابل *muqaabil/did*

age عمر *'umr*

AIDS أيدز *aydiz*

air conditioning تبريد *tabriid*

airmail بريد جوي *bariid jawwii*

air mattress سرير هوائي *sariir hawaa'ii*

airplane طائرة *taa'ira*

airport مطار *mataar*

alarm إنذار *indhaar*

alarm clock ساعة تنبيه *saa'at tanbiih*

alcohol خمر/كحول *kuhuul/khamr*

all day كل اليوم *kul al-yawm*

all the time طول الوقت *tuul al-waqt*

allergy حساسية *hassasiyya*

alone وحيدا *wahiidan*

altogether جميعا *jamii'an*

always دائما *daa'iman*

ambulance سيارة إسعاف *sayyaarat is'aaf*

America امريكا *amariikaa*

American امريكي *amariikii*

amount كمية *kammiyya*

amusement park حديقة *hadiiqa*

anesthetic (general) تخدير كامل *takhdiir kaamili*

anesthetic (local) تخدير موضعي *takhdiir mawdi'ii*

angry منفعل *munfa'il*

animal حيوان *hayawaan*

ankle كعب *ka'ib*

answer (رد) جواب *jawaab (rad)*

ant نمله *namla*

antibiotics مضاد حيوي *mudaad hayawii*

antifreeze مضاد للتجميد *mudaad lit-tajmiid*

antique قديم *qadiim*

antiques قديم *qadiim*

antiseptic مضاد للعفونة *mudaad lil-'ufuuna*

anus (المخرج) الشرج *ash-sharj (al-makhraj)*

apartment شقه للسكن *shaqqa lis-sakan*

aperitif مشهي *mushahhii*

apologies اعتذار *i'tidhaar*

apple تفاحة *tuffaaha*

apple juice عصير تفاح *'asiir tuffaah*

appointment موعد *maw'id*

April نيسان *naysaan*

architecture هندسة معمارية *handasa mi'maariya*

area منطقة/مساحة *masaaha/mintaqa*

area code ترقيم بريدي *tarqiim bariidii*

area code مفتاح المنطقة *miftaah al-mintaqa*

arm ذراع *dhiraa'*

arrange يرتب *yurattib*

arrive يصل *yasil*

arrow سهم *sahm*

art فن *fan*

art gallery معرض للفنون *ma'rad lil-funun*

artery شريان *sharayaan*

article مقال *maqaal*

artificial respiration التنفس الاصطناعي *at-tanaffus al-istinaa'ii*

ashtray منفضة سجائر *minfadat sajaa'ir*

ask يسال *yas'al*

ask for يطلب *yatlub*

aspirin اسبرين *asbariin*

assault اعتداء *i'tidaa'*

assorted مصنف *musannaf*

at home في البيت *fii al-bayt*

at night في الليل *fii al-layl*

at the back في الخلف *fii al-khalf*

at the front في الامام *fii al-amaam*

at the latest على الاقل *'alaa al-qal*

aubergine باذنجان *baadhinjaan*

August آب *aab*

Australia استراليا *ustiraaliyaa*

Australian استرالي *ustiraalii*

automatic اوتوماتيكي/ألي *aali/utumaatiikii*

autumn الخريف *al-khariif*

awake مستيقظ *mustayqiz*

awning الظل *az-zill*

B

baby رضيع/طفل *radii'/tifl*

baby food طعام طفل *ta'aam tifl*

babysitter حاضنة *haadina*

back (part of body) ظهر *zahr*

back (rear) خلف *khalf*

backpack حقيبة ظهر *haqibat zahr*

backpacker سائح مترجل *saa'ih mutarrajil*

bad (rotting) فاسد *faasid*

bad (terrible) سيء *sayyi'*

bag حقيبة *haqiiba*

baker خباز *khabbaaz*

balcony شرفة *shurfa*

ball كرة *kura*

ballpoint pen قلم جاف *qalam jaaf*

banana موز *mawz*

bandage ضماد *dimaad*

bandaids ضمادة *damaada*

bangs ضربة شديدة *darba shadiida*

bank (finance) مصرف *masraf*

bank (river) ضفة _diffa_

bar (café) بار _baar_

barbecue شواء في الهواء الطلق
shiwaa'fii al-hawaa' a<u>t</u>-<u>t</u>alq

basketball كرة السلة _kurat as-salla_

bath حمام _hammaam_

bathmat فرشة باب الحمام _far<u>sh</u>at
baab al-<u>h</u>ammaam_

bathrobe رداء حمام _ridaa' <u>h</u>ammam_

bathroom حمام _<u>gh</u>urfat al-hammaam_

bath towel منشفة حمام _min<u>sh</u>afat
<u>h</u>ammaam_

battery بطارية _ba<u>tt</u>aariya_

beach شبطئ _<u>sh</u>atii'_

beans فاصوليا _faa<u>s</u>uuliya_

beautiful جميل _jamiil_

bed فراش _firaa<u>sh</u>_

bedding مفروشات السرير
mafruu<u>sh</u>aat as-sariir

bee نحلة _na<u>h</u>la_

beef لحم بقر _la<u>h</u>m baqar_

beer بيرة _biira_

begin بيدأ _yabda'_

behind خلف _<u>kh</u>alf_

belt حزام _<u>h</u>izaam_

berth رصيف ميناء _ra<u>s</u>iif miinaa'_

better (to get) حسن _<u>h</u>asan_

bicycle دراجة هوائية _darraja hawaa'iyya_

bikini البيكيني _al-bikiinii_

bill فاتورة _fatuura_

billiards بليارد _bilyaard_

birthday عيد الميلاد _iid al-miilaad_

biscuit بسكويت _baskawiit_

bite لدغه _lad<u>gh</u>a_

bitter مر _mur_

black أسود _aswad_

black and white أسود و أبيض _aswad
wa abya<u>d</u>_

black eye عين سوداء _'ayn sawdaa'_

bland (taste) بلا طعم _bilaa <u>t</u>a'am_

blanket بطانية _ba<u>tt</u>aaniyya_

bleach مبيض _mubayyid_

bleed ينزف _yanzif_

blind (can't see) اعمى _a'maa_

blind (on window) ستارة _sitaara_

blister بثور جلدية _buthuur jildiyya_

blond اشقر _a<u>sh</u>kar_

blood دم _dam_

blood pressure ضغط الدم _da<u>gh</u>t
ad-dam_

bloody nose نزيف أنف _naziif anf_

blouse بلوزة _baluuza_

blue أزرق _azraq_

boat قارب _aqaarib_

body جسم _jism_

boiled مغلي _ma<u>gh</u>lii_

bone عظم _'a<u>z</u>m_

book كتاب _kitaab_

booked, reserved محجوز _ma<u>h</u>juuz_

booking office مكتب الحجز _maktab
hajz_

bookshop مكتبة _maktaba_

border حدود _huduud_

bored (ضجر) سئم _sa'im (dajir)_

boring ممل _mumil_

born مولود _mawluud_

borrow يستعير _yasta'iir_

botanic gardens حدائق نباتية
hadaa'iq nabaatiyya

both كلاهما _kilaahuma_

bottle (baby's) قنينة طفل _qinniinat <u>t</u>ifl_

bottle (wine) قنينة _qinniina_

bottle-warmer مسخن قنينة
musa<u>kh</u>in qinniina

box صندوق _<u>s</u>unduuq_

box office صندوق بريد _<u>s</u>unduuq bariid_

17

boy ولد *walad*

boyfriend صديق *sadiiq*

bra صدرية *sadriyya*

bracelet سوار *siwaar*

braised مطبوخ *matbukh*

brake مكابح/فرامل *faraamil/ makaabih*

brake oil زيت فرامل *zayt faraamil*

bread خبز *khubz*

break استراحة *istiraaha*

breakfast فطور *fatuur*

breast ثدي *thadii*

breast milk حليب ثدي *haliib thadii*

bridge جسر *jisr*

briefs ملخص *mulakhas*

bring يجلب *yajlib*

brochure منشور *manshuur*

broken عاطل/مكسور *maksuur/'aatil*

bronze نحاس/برونز *brunz/nuhaas*

broth حساء *hisaa'*

brother أخ *akh*

brown بني *bunnii*

bruise رضض *radad*

brush فرشاة *furshaat*

bucket سطل *satl*

buffet خزانة *khizaana*

bugs بق *baq*

building بناية *binaaya*

bun تسريحة *tasriiha*

burglary (سرقة) سطو *satw (sariqa)*

burn (injury) حرق *harq*

burn (verb) يحترق/يحرق *yuhriq/ yahtariq*

burnt محروق *mahruuq*

bus (باص) حافلة *haafila (baas)*

bus station (باصات) حافلات محطة *mahattat haafilaat (baasaat)*

bus stop (باص) حافلة موقف *mawkif haafila (baas)*

business card كارت *kaart*

business class أعمال درجة *darajat a'maal*

business trip عمل رحلة *rihlat 'amal*

busy (schedule) مشغول *mashghuul*

busy (traffic) ازدحام *izdihaam*

butane البوتان غاز *gaaz al-buutan*

butcher (جزار) قصاب *qassaab (jazaar)*

butter زبدة *zubda*

button زر *zirr*

by airmail الجوي بالبريد *bil-bariid al-jawwii*

by phone بالتليفون *bit-tilifuun*

C

cabbage ملفوف *malfuuf*

cabin كوخ *kuukh*

cake كعك *ka'k*

call (phonecall) مكالمة *mukaalama*

call (to phone) يتصل *yattasil*

called اتصل *ittasala*

camera كاميرا *kaamira*

camping مخيم *mukhayyam*

can opener علب مفتاح *miftaah 'ulab*

cancel يلغي *yulghii*

candle شمعة *sham'a*

candy حلوى *halwaa*

car سيارة *sayyaara*

car charger السيارة شاحن *shaahin al-saiyara*

cardigan صوف سترة *sutrat suuf*

car documents السيارة أوراق *awraaq as-sayyaara*

careful حذر *hadhir*

carpet سجادة *sajjaada*

carriage عربة 'araba

carrot جزر jazar

car seat (child's) مقعد طفل maq'ad tifl

cartridge خرطوشة khartuusha

car trouble عطب في السيارة 'atab fii as-sayyaara

cash نقدي/فلوس naqdii/fuluus

cash card بطاقة نقد bitaaqat naqd

cash desk مكتب تصريف maktab tasriif

cash machine آلة تصريف aalat tasriif

casino كازينو kaziinu

cassette شريط shariit

castle قلعة qal'a

cat قطة qitta

catalog كتالوغ katalugh

cauliflower قرنبيط qarnabiit

cause سبب sabab

cave كهف kahf

CD قرص qurs

CD-ROM مشغل أقراص mushaghil aqraas

celebrate يحتفل yahtafil

cell phone محمول/جوال mahmoul/jawwal

cemetery مقبرة maqbara

center (middle) مركز markaz

center (of city) مركز المدينة markaz al-madiina

centimeter سنتيميتر sintimitar

central heating تدفئة مركزية tadfi'a markaziyya

central locking قفل مركزي qifl markazii

certificate شهادة/وثيقة wathiiqa/shahaada

chair كرسي kursii

chambermaid خادمة فندق khaadima funduq

champagne شمبانيا shimbaaniya

change, swap يصرف yusarrif

change (money) صرف sarf

change (trains) تغير taghyiir

change the baby's diaper يغير حفاظ الطفل yughayyir haffaz ati-tifl

change the oil يغير الزيت yughayyir az-zayt

charger شاحن shaahin

charter flight رحلة جوية مؤجرة rihla jawwiyyaa mu'ajjara

chat دردشة dardasha

checked luggage فحص الحقائب fahs al-haqaa'ib

check, bill تدقيق tadqiiq

check (verb) فحص fahs

check in النزول بالفندق an-nuzuul bil-funduq

check out مغادرة الفندق mughadarat al-funduq

cheers! صحتين sahtiin

cheese جبن jubn

chef كبير الطباخين kabiir at-tabbaakhiin

chess شطرنج shitranj

chewing gum علك 'ilk

chicken دجاجة dajaaja

child طفل tifl

child's seat (in car) مقعد الطفل maq'ad tifl

chilled مثلج/مجمد mujammad/muthallaj

China ذقن dhaqn

chocolate شوكلاتة shuukalaata

choose اختار ikhtaar

chopsticks أعواد صينية a'waad siiniyya

church كنيسة *kaniisa*

church service صلاة الكنيسة <u>s</u>alaat al-kaniisa

cigar سيجار *siijaar*

cigarette سيجارة *siijaara*

circle دائرة *daa'ira*

circus سيرك *siirk*

citizen مواطن *muwaa<u>t</u>in*

city مدينة *madiina*

clean نظيف *na<u>z</u>iif*

clean (verb) ينظف *yuna<u>zz</u>if*

clearance (sale) تصفية *ta<u>s</u>fiya*

clock ساعة جدران *saa'at juduraan*

closed مغلق *mu<u>gh</u>laq*

closed off (road) مغلق *mu<u>gh</u>laq*

clothes ملابس *malaabis*

clothes hanger تعليقة ملابس *ta'liqah malaabis*

clothes dryer مجفف ملابس *mujaffif malaabis*

clothing ملابس/ثياب *malaabis/ thiyaab*

clutch (car) دواسة القابض *dawaasat l-qaabi<u>d</u>*

coat (jacket) سترة/جاكيت *jakiet/sitra*

coat (overcoat) معطف *mi'<u>t</u>af*

cockroach صرصور <u>s</u>ar<u>s</u>uur

cocoa كاكاو *kakaw*

coffee قهوه *qahwa*

cold (not hot) بارد *baarid*

cold, flu الإنفلونزا *influwanza*

collar باقة *baaqa*

collarbone الترقوة *at-turquwa*

colleague زميل *zamiil*

collision تصادم *tasaadum*

cologne عطر *'i<u>t</u>r*

color لون *lawn*

colored ملون *mulawwan*

comb مشط *mu<u>sh</u>t*

come تعال *ta'aala*

come back ارجع *irja'*

compartment (جناح) مقصورة *maksuura (jana<u>ah</u>)*

complaint شكوى *<u>sh</u>akwaa*

completely تماما *tamaaman*

compliment إكمال *ikmaal*

computer حاسوب/كمبيوتر *kambyuutar/<u>h</u>aasuub*

concert حفلة موسيقية *<u>h</u>afla muusiiqiyya*

concert hall قاعة غناء *qaa'at <u>gh</u>inaa'*

concierge حارس *<u>h</u>aaris*

concussion رجة *rajja*

condensed milk حليب مكثف *<u>h</u>aliib muka<u>th</u>af*

condom غطاء مطاطي *<u>gh</u>itaa' ma<u>tt</u>aa<u>t</u>ii*

confectionery حلويات *<u>h</u>alawiyyaat*

congratulations! مبروك/تهانينا *tahaaniinaa/mabruuk*

connection (transport) رحلة متممة *ri<u>h</u>la mutammima*

constipation قبض *qabi<u>d</u>*

consulate قنصلية *qun<u>s</u>iliyya*

consultation (by doctor) إستشارة *isti<u>sh</u>aara*

contact lens عدسات *'adasaat*

contagious معدي *mu'dii*

contraceptive pill حبوب منع الحمل *<u>h</u>ubuub man' al-<u>h</u>aml*

cook (person) طباخ *tabba<u>kh</u>*

cook (verb) يطبخ *ya<u>t</u>bu<u>kh</u>*

cookie بسكويت *baskawiit*

copper نحاسي *nu<u>h</u>aasii*

copy نسخة *nus<u>kh</u>a*

corkscrew مفتاح/مبرام *miftaa<u>h</u>/ mibraam*

corner ركن *rukn*

cornflower دقيق الذرة *daqiiq adh-dhura*

correct صحيح *sahiih*

correspond يراسل *yuraasil*

corridor ممر *mamar*

cosmetics مواد تجميل *mawaad tajmiil*

costume زي *zay*

cot سرير طفل *sariir tifl*

cotton قطن *qutn*

cotton wool صوف قطني *suuf qutnii*

cough كحة/سعال *su'aal/kahha*

cough (verb) يسعل (يكح) *yas'ul (yakuh)*

cough syrup شراب كحة *sharaab kahha*

counter ضد/عكس *'aks/did*

country (nation) بلد *balad*

country (rural area) ريف *riif*

country code الترقيم البريدي للبلد *at-tarqiim al-bariidii lil-balad*

courgette كوسة *kuusa*

course of treatment فترة علاج *fitrat 'ilaaj*

cousin ابن عم/بنت عم *ibn 'am/bint 'am*

crab سرطان البحر *sarataan al-bahr*

cracker كسارة *kassaara*

cream قشطة *qishta*

credit card بطاقة اعتماد *bitaaqat i'timaad*

crime جريمة *jariima*

crockery ادوات فخارية *adawaat fakhariyya*

cross (road, river) تقاطع *taqaatu'*

crossroad تقاطع طرق *taqaatu' turuq*

crutch عكاز *'ukkaaz*

cry بكاء *bukaa'*

cubic meter متر مكعب *mitr muka'ab*

cucumber خيار *khiyaar*

cuddly toy لعبة مسلية *lu'ba musalliya*

cuff الكم *al-kumm*

cufflinks زر كم القميص *zirr kum al-qamiis*

cup كوب *kuub*

curly مجعد *muja'ad*

current (electric) تيار *tayyaar*

curtains ستائر *sataa'ir*

cushion وسادة *wisaada*

custom عادة *'aada*

customs جمارك *jamaarik*

cut (injury) جرح *jurh*

cut (verb) يقطع *yaqta'*

cutlery لوازم المائدة *lawaazim al-maa'ida*

cycling سباق الدراجات *sibaaq ad-darraajaat*

D

dairy products لبنيات *labaniyyaat*

damage ضرر (خراب) *darar (kharaab)*

dance يرقص *yarqus*

dandruff قشرة *qishra*

danger خطر *khatar*

dangerous خطير *khatiir*

dark ظلام *zalaam*

date تاريخ *taariikh*

date of birth تاريخ الميلاد *taariikh miilaad*

daughter بنت *bint*

day يوم *yawm*

day after tomorrow بعد غد *ba'da ghad*

day before yesterday امس الأول *amsi al-awwal*

dead ميت *mayyit*

deaf اطرش *atrash*

decaffeinated خال من الكافايين *khaalin min l-kaafiin*

December كانون الاول *kaanuun ath-thaanii*

declare (customs) يصرح *yusarrih*

deep عميق *'amiiq*

deep freeze تجمد عميق *tajammud 'amiiq*

deep-sea diving الغوص في أعماق البحار *al-ghaws fii a'maaq al-bihaar*

defecate يتغوط *yataghawwat*

degrees درجات *darajaat*

delay تأخير *ta'khiir*

delicious لذيذ *ladhiidh*

dentist طبيب أسنان *tabiib asnaan*

dentures طقم اسنان *taqum asnaan*

deodorant معطر *mu'attir*

department store محل تجاري *mahall tijaarii*

departure مغادرة *mughaadara*

departure time وقت المغادرة *waqt al-mughaadara*

depilatory cream مستحضر مزيل الشعر *mustahdir muziil lish-sha'r*

deposit (for safekeeping) وديعة/أمانة *amaana/wadii'a*

deposit (in bank) يودع *yuudi'*

desert صحراء *sahraa'*

dessert حلويات *halawiyyaat*

destination مقصد/مصير *masiir/maqsad*

detergent مادة مطهرة *maadda mutahhira*

develop (photo) تحميض *tahmiid*

diabetic سكري *sukkarii*

dial طلب رقم على الهاتف *talab raqm 'alaa al-haatif*

diamond ألماس *almaas*

diaper حفاظ طفل *haffaz tifl*

diarrhea اشهال *ishhaal*

dictionary قاموس *qaamuus*

diesel oil زيت الديزل *zayt ad-diizil*

diet غذاء *ghidhaa'*

difficulty صعوبة *su'uuba*

dining car عربة طعام *'arabat ta'aam*

dining room غرفة الطعام *ghurfat at-ta'aam*

dinner عشاء *'ashaa'*

direction إتجاه *ittijaah*

direct flight طيران مباشر *tayaraan mubaashir*

directly مباشر *mubaasharatan*

dirty وسخ *wasikh*

disabled معاق *mu'aaq*

disco ديسكو *diskuu*

discount تخفيض *takhfiid*

dish طبق/صحن *sahin/tabaq*

dish of the day طبق اليوم *tabaq al-yawm*

disinfectant مبيد حشرات *mubid hasharaat*

distance مسافة *masaafa*

distilled water ماء مقطر *maa' muqattar*

disturb يزعج *yuz'ij*

disturbance ازعاج *iz'aaj*

dive يغوص *yaghuus*

diving غطس *ghats*

diving board منصة الغوص *manassat al-ghaws*

diving gear لاوازم الغوص *lawaazim al-ghaws*

divorced مطلق *mutallaq*

dizzy (دوخة) دوار *duwaar (dawha)*

do يعمل *ya'mal*

doctor طبيب _t_abiib

dog كلب kalb

do-it-yourself store محل خدمات ذاتية ma_h_al _kh_adamaat _dh_aatiyya

doll دمية dumiya

domestic محلي ma_h_allii

done (cooked) مطبوخ ma_t_buu_kh_

do not disturb الرجاء عدم الإزعاج ar-rajaa' 'adam al-izaaj

door باب baab

double ضعف _di_'f

down اسفل asfal

download تحميل ta_h_miil

drapes ستائر sataa'ir

draught جفاف jafaaf

dream (verb) يحلم yahlum

dress يلبس/بدلة badla/yalbas

dressing gown عباءة 'abaa'a

dressing table منضدة min_d_ada

drink (alcoholic) خمر (مشروب) _kh_amr (ma_shruub_)

drink (refreshment) شراب _sh_araab

drink (verb) يشرب ya_sh_rab

drinking water ماء شرب maa' _sh_urb

drive يسوق yasuuq

driver سائق saa'iq

driver's license رخصة سياقة ru_kh_sat siyaaqa

drugstore مخزن ادوية ma_kh_zan adwiya

drunk سكران sakraan

dry جاف jaaf

dry (verb) يجفف/يجف yujaffif/yajuf

dry-clean غسل وتجفيف _gh_asl wa tajfiif

drycleaners غسل جاف _gh_asl jaff

duck بطة ba_tt_a

during خلال _kh_ilaal

during the day خلال اليوم _kh_ilaal al-yawm

duty (tax) رسم جمركي rasm jumrukii

duty-free goods بضائع غير خاضعة للرسم الجمركي badaa'i' _gh_ayr _kh_aa_d_i'a lir-rasm al-jumrukii

duty-free shop دكان غير خاضع للرسم الجمركي dukaan _kh_aa_d_i' lir-rasm al-jumrukii

DVD دي في دي dii vii dii

E

ear أذن u_dh_un

earache ألم في الاذن alam fii al-u_dh_un

ear drops قترة للاذن qatra lil-u_dh_un

early مبكر mubakkir

earrings الدخل da_kh_l

earth أرض ar_d_

earthenware خزف _kh_azaf

east شرق _sh_arq

easy سهل sahl

eat يأكل ya'kul

economy class درجة اقتصادية daraja iqti_s_aadiyya

eczema اكزما akzima

eel سمكة الأنقليس samakat al-anqaliis

egg بيض bay_d_

eggplant باذنجان baa_dh_injaan

electric كهربائي kahrabaa'ii

electricity كهرباء kahrabaa'

electronic الكتروني ilikituunii

elephant فيل fiil

elevator مصعد كهربائي mis'ad kahrabaa'ii

email بريد إلكتروني bariid iliktoronii

embassy سفارة saraara

embroidery تطريز ta_t_riiz

emergency brake مكابح طوارئ makaabih _t_awaari'

emergency exit مخرج طوارىء *makhraj tawaari'*

emergency phone هاتف طوارىء *haatif tawaari'*

emperor امبراطور *imbiraatuur*

empress امبراطورة *imbiraatuura*

empty فارغ *faarigh*

engaged (on the phone) مشغول *mashguul*

engaged (to be married) مخطوبة/مخطوب *makhtuub/ makhtuuba*

England انجلترا *ingiltaraa*

English انجليزي *ingliizii*

enjoy يتمتع *yatamatta'*

enquire استفسار/يستفسر *istifsaar/ yastafsir*

envelope ظرف *zarf*

escalator درج ميكانيكي *daraj miikaaniikii*

escort يرافق *yuraafiq*

essential اساسي *asaasii*

evening مساء *masaa'*

evening wear لباس المساء *libaas al-masaa'*

event مناسبة/حدث *hadath/ munaasaba*

everything كل شيء *kull shay'*

everywhere في كل مكان *fii kull makaan*

examine يفحص *yafhas*

excavation تنقيب *tanqiib*

excellent ممتاز *mumtaasz*

exchange يصرف/يبدل عملة *yubaddil 'amila/yusarrif*

exchange office مكتب تصريف *maktab tasriif*

excursion رحلة *rihla*

exhibition معرض *ma'rad*

exit مخرج *maqraj*

expenses مصاريف/نفقات *masaariif/ nafaqaat*

expensive غال *ghaalin*

explain يشرح *yashrah*

express يعبر *ya'bur*

external خارجي *khaarijii*

eye عين *ayn*

eye drops قطرة للعين *qatra lil-ayn*

eye specialist أخصائي عيون *akhissaa'ii uyuun*

F

fabric قماش *qumaash*

face وجه *wajh*

Facebook فايس بوك *Facebook*

factory مصنع *masna'*

fall (season) خريف *khariif*

fall (verb) يسقط *yasqut*

family عائلة *'aa'ila*

famous مشهور *mashhuur*

fan مروحة *marwaha*

far away بعيد *baiid*

farm مزرعة *mazra'a*

farmer فلاح *fallah*

fashion زي *zay*

fast سريع *sarii'*

father اب *ab*

father-in-law الحمو *al-hamuw*

fault خطأ *khata'*

fax فاكس *faaks*

February شباط *shubaat*

feel يشعر *yash'ur*

feel like يود *yawadd*

fence سور *suur*

ferry عبارة/سفينة *safiina/'abbaara*

fever حرارة/حمى *hummaa/haraara*

fiancé خطيب _kh_atiib

fiancée خطيبة _kh_atiiba

fill يملأ yamla'

filling (dental) حشوة _h_ashwa

filling (in food) مملوء mamluu'

fill out (form) يملأ yamla'

film (cinema) فلم film

film (photo) فلم film

filter (فلتر) مصفاة mi_s_faat (filtar)

filter cigarette سيجار فلتر sijaar filtar

fine (good) (حسن) جيد jayyid (_h_asan)

fine (money) خطية/غرامة _gh_araama/_kh_atiyya

finger إصبع i_s_bi'

fire حريق/نار naar/_h_riiq

fire alarm منبه حريق munabbih _h_ariiq

fire department الاطفاء al-itfaa'

fire escape مهرب حريق mahrab _h_ariiq

fire extinguisher آلة اطفاء النار aalat i_t_faa' al-naar

first اول awwal

first aid اسعافات اولية is'aafaat awwaliyya

first class درجة أولى daraja uulaa

fish سمك samak

fish (verb) يصطاد السمك yas_t_aad as-samak

fishing rod عصا الصيد 'a_s_aa a_s_-_s_ayd

fitness club نادي لياقة naadii liyaaqa

fitness training تدريب لياقة tadriib liyaaqa

fitting room غرفة المقاييس _gh_urfat al-maqaayiis

fix (puncture) يصلح yu_s_lih

flag علم 'alam

flash (camera) (فلاش) ضوء _d_aw' (fla_sh_)

flashlight ضوء متقطع _d_aw' mutaqa_tt_i'

flatulence تطبيل ta_t_biil

flavor نكهة nukha

flavoring مادة منكهة maadda munakkiha

flea برغوث bar_gh_uuth

flea market سوق البرغوث suuq al-bar_gh_uuth

flight رحلة طيران ri_h_lat _t_ayaraan

flight number رقم الرحلة raqam ar-ri_h_la

flood فيضان faya_d_aan

floor أرضية/طابق ar_d_iyya/_t_aabaq

flour طحين ta_h_iin

flu الإنفلونزا al-influwanza

flush (verb) تغسل ya_gh_sil

fly (insect) ذبابة _dh_ubaaba

fly (verb) يطير ya_t_iir

fog ضباب _d_abaab

foggy ضبابي _d_abaabii

folklore فلكلور fuliklor

follow يتبع yatba'

food (groceries) مواد غذائية mawaad _gh_idhaa'iyya

food (meal) (غذاء) طعام ta'aam (_gh_idhaa')

food court ساحة مطاعم saa_h_at mataa'im

food poisoning تسمم غذائي tasammum _gh_idhaa'ii

foot قدم qadam

foot brake كسر القدم kasr al-qadam

forbidden يمنع/يحرم yu_h_arrim/yamna'

forehead جبين jabiin

foreign أجنبي/غريب _gh_ariib/ajnabii

forget ينسى yansaa

fork شوكة _sh_awka

form استمارة istimaara

formal dress زي رسمي *zay rasmii*

forward (letter) يرسل *yusrsil*

fountain نافورة *nafuura*

frame أطار *iṭaar*

free (no charge) مجاني *majjaanii*

free (unoccupied) حر *ḥur*

free time وقت فراغ *waqt faraagh*

freeze (التجمد) التجمد *injimaad*

french fries مقليات فرنسية *maqliyyat faransiyya*

fresh طازج *ṭaazij*

Friday الجمعة *al-jumu'a*

fried مقلي *maqlii*

friend صديق *sadiiq*

friendly ودي *widdii*

frightened مذعور *madh'uur*

fringe (hair) القصة *al-qussa*

frozen مجمد *mujammad*

fruit فواكه *fawaakih*

fruit juice عصير فواكه *'aṣiir fawaaqih*

frying pan مقلاة *maqlaat*

full مملوء/شبعان *shab'aan/mamluu'*

fun مرح/لهو *marah/lahw*

funeral جنائز *janaa'iz*

G

gallery بهو (صالة) *bahw (ṣaala)*

game لعبة *lu'ba*

garage (car repair) ورشة تصليح *warshat taṣliih*

garbage زبالة *zibaala*

garlic ثوم *thuum*

garden حديقة *ḥadiiqa*

garment ثوب *thawb*

gas (for heating) غاز *ghaaz*

gasoline بنزين *banziin*

gas station محطة وقود *maḥaṭṭat waquud*

gate بوابة *bawwaaba*

gear (car) التروس *at-turuus*

gem جوهرة *jawhara*

gender الجنس *al-jins*

get off يخرج/ينزل *yakhruj/yanzil*

get on يصعد *yas'ad*

gift هدية *hadiyya*

ginger زنجبيل *zanjabiil*

girl بنت *bint*

girlfriend صديقة *sadiiqa*

given name الاسم *al-ism*

glass (for drinking) كأس/كوب *kuub/ka's*

glass (material) زجاج *zujaaj*

glasses نظارات *nazzaaraat*

gliding طيران شراعي *ṭayaraan shiraa'ii*

glossy (photo) لامع *laami'*

gloves قفازات *quffaazaat*

glue صمغ *samagh*

gnat بعوضة *ba'uuda*

go اذهب *idhhab*

go back ارجع *irji'*

go out اخرج *ukhruj*

gold ذهب *dhahab*

golf صولجان/غولف *gulf/sawlajaan*

golf course ملعب الغولف *mal'ab al-gulf*

good afternoon مساء الخير *massa' al-khayr*

goodbye مع السلامة *ma'a as-salaama*

good evening مساء الخير *massa' al-khayr*

good morning صباح الخير *sabaah al-khayr*

good night تصبح على خير *tuṣbih 'alaa khayr*

goose أوزة iwazza

Global Positioning System (GPS) نظام تحديد الموقع العالمي (جي بي إس) nizaam tahdiid al-mawaqi' al-'alamii (GPS)

gram غرام ghraam

grandchild حفيد hafiid

granddaughter حفيدة hafiida

grandfather جد jad

grandmother جدة jadda

grandparent الجدان al-jaddaan

grandson حفيد hafiid

grape juice عصير عنب 'asiir 'inab

grapes عنب 'inab

grave مقبرة maqbara

gray رمادي ramaadii

graze (injury) يرعى yar'aa

greasy مشحم mushahham

green أخضر akhdar

greengrocer خضار khaddaar

greeting تحية tahiyya

grey-haired ذو شعر رمادي dhuu sha'r ramaadii

grilled مشوي mashwii

grocer بقال baqqaal

groceries بقالة biqaala

group مجموعة majmuu'a

guest house بيت ضيافة bayt diyaafa

guide (book) دليل daliil

guide (person) مرشد/موجه muwajjih/murshid

guided tour رحلة مع مرشد rihla ma'a murshid

guilt إثم/ذنب dhanb/ithm

gym جمناستك jumnaastik

gynecologist أخصائي أمراض النساء akhissaii amraad an-nisaa'

H

hair شعر sha'r

hairbrush مشط mushit

haircut قصة شعر qassat sha'r

hairdresser حلاق hallaaq

hairdryer مجفف شعر mujaffif sha'r

hairspray رشاش شعر rashaash sha'r

hairstyle تسريحة شعر tasriihat sha'r

half نصف nisf

half full نصف مملوء nisf mamluu'

hammer مطرقة mitraqa

hand يد yad

handbag حقيبة يد haqiibat yad

hand brake فرامل يدوية fraamil yadawiyya

handkerchief منديل mindiil

hand luggage حقيبة يد haqiiba yad

handmade صنع يدوي sun' yadawii

hand towel منشفة minshafa

happy سعيد sa'iid

harbor ميناء minaa'

hard (difficult) صعب sa'b

hard (firm) قاسي/صلب salb/qaasii

hardware store متجر مواد معدنية matjar mawaad ma'daniyya

hat قبعة qubba'a

hay fever حمى القش humma al-qash

head رأس ra's

headache صداع sudaa'

headlights إضاءة أمامية idaa'a amaamiyya

health food shop دكان اطعمة صحية dukkaan at'ima sihhiyya

healthy صحي sihhii

hear يسمع yasma'

hearing aid سماعات اذن sammaa'aat udhun

heart قلب qalb

heart attack أزمة قلبية azma qalbiyya

heat حرارة haraara

heater مدفأة midfa'a

heavy ثقيل thaqiil

heel (of foot) كعب ka'b

heel (of shoe) كعب ka'b

hello اهلا ahlan

help النجدة/مساعدة musaa'ada/ an-najda

helping (of food) معونة ma'uuna

hem حافة haafat

herbal tea شاي الاعشاب shaay al-'ashaab

herbs اعشاب 'ashaab

here هنا hunaa

high عال 'aalin

high chair كرسي عال للأطفال kursii 'aalii lil-atfaal

high tide أعلى مستوى للمد a'laa mustawaa lil-mad

highway طريق سريع tariiq sarii'

hiking نزهة سير على الاقدام nuzhat sayr 'alaa al-aqdaam

hiking boots حذاء نزهة السير على الاقدام hidhaa' nuzhat as-sayr 'alaa al-aqdaam

hip ورك warak

hire يستأجر yasta'jir

hitchhike سفر تطفلي safar tataffulii

hobby هواية hiwaaya

holdup توقف tawaqquf

holiday (festival) عطلة 'utla

holiday (public) عطلة 'utla

holiday (vacation) إجازة ijaaza

homesick الحنين إلى الوطن al-haniin ila l-watan

honest أمين amiin

honey عسل 'asal

horizontal أفقي ufuqii

horrible كريه kariih

horse حصان hisaan

hospital مستشفى mustashfaa

hospitality ضيافة diyaafa

hot (bitter, sharp) حاد haad

hot (warm) حار haar

hot spring ربيع حار rabii' haar

hot-water bottle قنينة ماء حار qinniinat maa' haar

hotel فندق funduq

hour ساعة saa'a

house بيت bayt

houses of parliament مقر البرلمان maqar al-barlamaan

how? كيف؟ kayf?

how far? كم المسافة؟ kam al-masaafa?

how long? كم المدة؟ kam al-mudda?

how many? كم؟ kam?

how much? كم؟ kam?

hundred grams مئة غرام mi'at ghraam

hungry جائع (جوعان) jaa'i' (jaw'aan)

hurry بسرعة/أسرع asri'/bisur'a

husband زوج zawj

hut كوخ kuukh

I

ice cream بوظة buuza

ice cubes مكعبات ثلج muka'abaat thalj

iced مثلج muthallaj

ice-skating تزلج على الجليد tazalluj 'alaa ath-thalj

idea فكرة fikra

identification (card) بطاقة شخصية bitaaqa shakhsiyya

identify يتعرف *yuta'arraf*

ignition key مفتاح قدح *miftaah qadh*

ill مريض *mariid*

illness مرض *marad*

imagine يتخيل *yatakhayyal*

immediately حالا *haalan*

important مهم *muhim*

import duty ضريبة الاستيراد *dariibat al-istiiraad*

impossible مستحيل *mustahiil*

improve يحسن/يطور *yutawwir/ yuhassin*

in في *fii*

indigestion سوء هضم *suu' hadm*

in-laws الأنساب *al-ansaab*

in the evening في المساء *fii al-masaa'*

in the morning في الصباح *fii as-sabaah*

included مشمول *mashmuul*

include in يشمل *yashmal*

indicate يوضح *yuwaddih*

indicator (car) إشارة *ishaara*

inexpensive رخيص *rakhiis*

infection إلتهاب *iltihaab*

infectious معدي *mu'dii*

inflammation التهاب *iltihaab*

information معلومات *ma'luumaat*

information office مكتب معلومات *maktab ma'luumaat*

injection حقنة *huqna*

injured مجروح *majruuh*

inner tube أنبوب داخلي *unbuub dakhilii*

innocent بريء *barii'*

insect حشرة *hashara*

insect bite لدغة حشرة *ladghat hashara*

insect repellant مبيد حشرة *mubiid hashara*

inside داخل *daakhil*

install تثبيت *tathbiit*

instructions تعليمات *ta'liimaat*

insurance تأمين/ضمان *damaan/ ta'miin*

intermission فترة استراحة *fitrat istiraaha*

internal داخلي *daakhilii*

international دولي *duwalii*

Internet إنترنت *Internet*

Internet café (cyber) مقهى إنترنت (سايبر) *maqha internet (saybar)*

interpreter مترجم *mutarjim*

intersection تقاطع *taqaatu'*

introduce oneself يقدم (يعرف) *yuqaddim (yu'arrif)*

invite يدعو *yad'uu*

invoice فاتورة *faatuura*

iodine اليود *al-yuud*

Ireland ايرلندا *iirlanda*

iron (metal) حديد *hadiid*

iron (for clothes) مكواة *mikwaat*

iron (verb) يكوي *yakwii*

ironing board لوح الكوي *lawh kawii*

island جزيرة *jaziira*

itch حكة *hakka*

⟨ج⟩

jack (for car) رافعة *raafi'a*

jacket (سترة) جاكيت *jaakiit (sutra)*

jam مربى *murabba*

January كانون الثاني *kanuun ath-thaanii*

jaw فك *fak*

jeans جينز *jeanz*

jellyfish قنديل البحر *qindiil al-bahr*

jeweler صائغ *saa'igh*

jewelry مجوهرات *mujawharaat*

job شغل/وظيفة shughl/waziifa

jog يركض yarkud

joke نكتة nukta

journey رحلة rihla

juice عصير 'asiir

July تموز tammuuz

June حزيران huzayraan

junk mail البريد غير المرغوب فيه al-bariid ghiir marghoub fiih

K

kerosene كيروسين kiirusiin

key مفتاح miftaah

kidney الكلى al-kilaa

kilogram كيلوغرام kiloghraam

king ملك malik

kiss قبلة qubla

kiss (verb) يقبل yuqabbil

kitchen مطبخ matbakh

knee ركبة rukba

knife سكين sikiin

knit يحوك yahuuk

know يعرف ya'rif

L

lace (fabric) زخرفة zakhrafa

laces (for shoes) رباط حذاء ribaata al-hidhaa'

ladder درج daraj

lake بحيرة buhayra

lamb (حمل) خروف kharuuf (haml)

lamp مصباح misbaah

land (ground) أرض ard

land (verb) (تنزل) تحط tahut (tanzil)

lane (of traffic) مسار masaar

language لغة lugha

laptop حاسوب محمول hasoub mahmoul

large (واسع) كبير kabiir (waasi')

last (endure) يستمر yastamir

last (final) آخر aakhir

last night الليلة الماضية al-layla al-maadiya

late متأخر muta'akhir

later فيما بعد fiimaa ba'd

laugh يضحك yadhak

launderette مؤسسة غسل وكوي mu'assat ghasl wa kawii

laundry soap صابون ملابس saabun malaabis

law قانون qaanuun

lawyer محامي muhaamii

laxative (ملين) مسهل musahil (mulayyin)

leak تسرب tasarrub

leather جلد jild

leather goods بضائع جلدية badaa'i' jildiyya

leave يغادر yughaadir

left يسار/متبقي mutabaqqii/yasaar

left behind نسي nasiya

leg ساق saaq

leggings غطاء الساقين ghitaa' as-saaqayn

leisure وقت فراغ waqt

lemon ليمون laymuun

lend يقرض yuqrid

lens (camera) عدسات 'adasaat

less أقل aqal

lesson درس dars

letter حرف/رسالة risaala/harf

lettuce خس khass

level crossing معبر ma'bar

library مكتبة maktaba

license إجارة/رخصة rukhsa/ijaaza

lie (be lying) يكذب *yakdhib*

lie (falsehood) كذب *kadhib*

lie down يستلقي *yastalqii*

lift (elevator) مصعد *mis'ad*

lift (in car) توصيلة *tawsiila*

light (lamp) مصباح *misbah*

light (not dark) مضيء *mudii'*

light (not heavy) خفيف *khafiif*

light bulb مصباح *misabah*

lighter قداحة *qiddaha*

lightning البرق *al-barq*

like (verb) يحب (يرغب) *yuhib (yarghab)*

line خط *khat*

linen كتان *kittaan*

lining بطانة *bitaana*

liquor store مخزن مشروبات *makhzan mashruubaat*

liqueur مشروبات كحولية *mashruubaat kuhuuliyya*

listen يصغي (يستمع) *yusghii (yastami')*

liter لتر *latr*

literature أدب *adab*

little (amount) قليل *qaliil*

little (small) صغير *saghiir*

live (alive) يعيش *ya'iish*

live (verb) يسكن *yaskun*

liver الكبد *al-kabid*

lobster جراد البحر *jaraad al-bahr*

local محلي *mahallii*

lock قفل/يقفل *qufl/yaqfil*

long طويل *tawiil*

long-distance call مكالمة بعيدة *maukama ba'iida*

look at ينظر الى *yanzur ilaa*

look for يبحث عن *yabhath 'an*

look-up يبحث عن *yabhath 'an*

lose يفقد *yafqid*

loss خسارة (فقدان) *khasaara (fiqdaan)*

lost (can't find way) مفقود *mafquud*

lost (missing) ضائع *daa'i*

lost and found office مكتب الموجودات والمفقودات *maktab al-mawjuudaat wa al-mafquudaat*

lotion مستحضر غسيل *mustahdar ghasiil*

loud عال *'aalin*

love حب *hub*

love (verb) يحب *yuhib*

low منخفض *munkhafid*

low tide ادنى مستوى للجزر *adnaa mustawaa lil-jazr*

LPG غاز *ghaz*

luck حظ *haz*

luggage حقائب/امتعة *amti'a/haqaa'ib*

luggage locker خزانة الحقائب *khizaanat al-haqaa'ib*

lumps (sugar) قطع السكر *qita' as-sukkar*

lunch غداء *ghidhaa'*

lungs الرئتان *ar-ri'ataan*

M

madam مدام (سيدة) *madam (sayyida)*

magazine مجلة *majalla*

mail (letters) بريد *bariid*

mail (verb) يرسل بالبريد *yursil bil-bariid*

main post office مكتب البريد الرئيسي *maktab al-briid ar-ra'iisii*

main road طريق رئيسي *tariiq ra'iisii*

make, create يخلق/يصنع *yasna'/yakhlaq*

make an appointment يحدد موعدا *yuhaddid maw'idan*

make love الجنس يمارس *yumaaris al-jins*

makeshift مؤقت بديل *badiil mu'aqqat*

makeup مكياج *mikyaaj*

man رجل *rajul*

manager مدير *mudiir*

mango مانجا *manja*

manicure اظافر صبغ *subgh azaafir*

many كثير *kathiir*

map خارطة *khaarita*

marble مرمر *marmar*

March آذار *aadhaar*

margarine زبدة *zubda*

marina مرسى *marsaa*

marital status المدنية الحالة *al-haala al-madaniyya*

market سوق *suuq*

married متزوج *mutazawwij*

mass كتلة *kutla*

massage رسالة *risaala*

mat (on floor) صغيرة سجادة *sajaada saghiira*

mat (on table) الطاولة قماش قطعة *qit'at qumaash at-taawila*

match (يناسب) يوافق *yuwaafiq (yunaasib)*

matches كبريت *kabriit*

May أيار *ayaar*

maybe ربما *rubbamaa*

mayonnaise مايونيز *maayuuniiz*

mayor محافظ *muhaafiz*

meal غذائية وجبة *wajba ghidhaa'iyya*

mean يعني *ya'nii*

measure يقيس *yaqiis*

measuring jug مكيال *mikyaal*

measure out يقيس *yaqiis*

meat لحم *lahm*

medication علاج *'ilaaj*

medicine دواء *dawaa'*

meet ب يلتقي *yaltaqii bi*

melon (شمام) بطيخ *battikh (shimmaam)*

member عضو *'udw*

member of parliament برلمان عضو *'udw barlamaan*

membership card عضوية بطاقة *bitaaqat 'udwiyya*

mend يصلح/تصليح *yuslih/tasliih*

menstruate تحيض *tahiid*

menstruation حيض *hayd*

menu المأكولات قائمة *qaa'imat al-ma'kuulaat*

message رسالة *risaala*

metal معدن *ma'dan*

meter متر *matr*

meter (in taxi) عداد *'addad*

migraine الشقيقة صداع *sudaa' ash-shaqiiqa*

mild (taste) لطيف *latiif*

milk حليب *haliib*

millimeter مليمتر *millimitr*

mineral water معدنية مياه *miyaah ma'daniyya*

minute دقيقة *daqiiqa*

mirror مراة *mir'aat*

miss (flight, train) عن يتأخر *yata'akhar 'an*

miss (loved one) يشتاق *yashtaaq*

missing مفقود *mafquud*

missing person مفقود شخص *shakhis mafquud*

mist ضباب *dabaab*

misty غامض *ghamid*

mistake (غلطة) خطا *khata' (ghalta)*

mistaken مخطيء *mukhti'*

misunderstanding سوء فهم suu' fahm

mixed ممزوج mamzuuj

modern art الفن الحديث al-fan al-hadiith

moment لحظة lahza

monastery دير dayr

Monday الاثنين al-ithnayn

money (فلوس) نقود nuquud (fuluus)

monkey قرد qird

month شهر shahr

moon قمر qamr

moped دراجة آلية darraaja aaliya

mosquito بعوضة ba'uuda

mosquito net شبكة بعوض shabakat ba'uud

motel فندق صغير fundiq saghiir

mother ام um

mother-in-law الحماة al-hamaa

motorbike دراجة نارية darraaja naariya

motorboat زورق مزود بمحرك zawraq muzawwad bi-muharrak

mountain جبل jabal

mountain hut كوخ جبلي kuukh jabalii

mouse فأر fa'r

mouth فم fam

MSG رسالة risaala

much كثير kathiir

mud طين tiin

muscle عضلة 'adala

muscle spasms تقلص عضلي taqallus 'adalii

museum متحف mathaf

mushrooms الفطر al-futr

music موسيقى muusiiqaa

N

nail (finger) ظفر zifr

nail (metal) مسمار mismaar

nail file مبرد اظافر mibrad azaafir

nail scissors مقص اظافر miqas azaafir

naked عار 'aarin

nappy, diaper حفاظ طفل haffaz tifl

nationality جنسية jinsiyya

natural طبيعي tabii'ii

nature طبيعة tabii'a

nauseous مقرف muqurif

near قرب qurb

nearby قريب qariib

necessary ضروري daruurii

neck رقبة raqaba

necklace قلادة qilaada

necktie ربطة عنق rabtat 'unuq

needle إبرة ibra

negative (photo) نيجاتيف الصور nijaatiif as-suwar

neighbor جار jaar

nephew ابن الاخت/ابن الاخ ibn al-akh/ibn al-ukht

never أبد abadan

new جديد jadiid

news أخبار akhbaar

newspaper صحيفة/جريدة sahiifa/ jariida

news stand كشك الصحف kushik as-suhuf

next اللاحق/القادم al-laahiq/al-qaadim

next to بالقرب من bilqurb

nice (person) (جميل) طيب tayyib (jamiil)

nice (pleasant) (ممتع) جميل jamiil (mumti')

niece بنت الاخت/بنت الاخ bint al-akh/ bint al-ukht

night ليل *layl*

night duty دوام ليلي *dawaam laylii*

nightclothes ملابس ليلية *malaabis layliyya*

nightclub نادي ليلي *naadii laylii*

nightdress لباس ليلي *libas laylii*

nipple (bottle) حلمة *hilma*

no لا/كلا *laa/kallaa*

no entry ممنوع الدخول *mamnuu' ad-dukhuul*

no thank you لا شكرا لك *laa shukran laka*

noise ضوضاء *dawdaa'*

nonstop (flight) دون توقف *duun tawaqquf*

noodles معكرونة *ma'karuuna*

no-one لا احد *laa ahad*

normal طبيعي *tabii'ii*

north شمال *shamaal*

nose انف *anf*

nosebleed نزيف الانف *naziif anf*

nose drops قطرة انف *qatrat anf*

notebook دفتر ملاحظات *daftar mulaahazaat*

notepad ورق ملاحظات *waraq mulaahazaat*

notepaper دفتر ملاحظات *daftar mulaahazaat*

nothing لا شيء *laa shay'*

November تشرين الثاني *tishriin ath-thaanii*

nowhere ليس في أي مكان *laysa fii ay-makaan*

number رقم *raqim*

number plate رقم السيارة *raqim as-sayyaara*

nurse ممرضة *mumarrida*

nuts فستق *fustuq*

O

occupation وظيفة (شغل) *waziifa (shughl)*

October تشرين الأول *tishriin al-awwal*

off (gone bad) فاسد *faasid*

off (turned off) يغلق (يطفيء) *yughliq (yutfi')*

offer عرض *ard*

office دائرة *daa'ira*

oil زيت *zayt*

oil level مستوى الزيت *mustawaa az-zayt*

ointment مرهم *marham*

okay نعم/لا بأس *laa ba's/naam*

old قديم *qadiim*

on, at عند/على *'alaa/inda*

on (turned on) مشغل/مفتوح *maftuuh/musahghal*

on board راكب *raakib*

oncoming car سيارة قادمة *sayyaara qaadima*

one-way ticket تذكرة سفر رحلة واحدة *tadhkirat safar rihla waahida*

one-way traffic حركة مرور باتجاه واحد *harakat muruur bit-tijaah waahid*

onion بصل *basal*

on the left على اليسار *'alaa al-yasaar*

on the right على اليمين *'alaa al-yamiin*

on the way في الطريق *fii at-tariiq*

open مفتوح *maftuuh*

open (verb) يفتح *yaftah*

operate (surgeon) عملية جراحية *'amaliyya jiraahiyya*

operator (telephone) العامل بمركز الإتصالات *al-'aamil bi-markaz al-ittisaalaat*

opposite مقابل/عكس *'aks/muqaabul*

optician نظاراتي *nadhaaraatii*

orange (color) برتقالي *burtughalii*

orange (fruit) برتقال *butughaal*

order رتبة/(طلب) أمر *amr (talab)/ rutba*

order (verb) يأمر *ya'mur*

other آخر *aakhar*

other side من جهة أخرى *min jiha ukhraa*

outside خارج *khaarij*

overpass معبر *ma'bar*

overseas في الخارج *fii al-khaarij*

overtake يتجاوز *yatajaawaz*

over there هناك *hunaak*

oyster محار *mahhaar*

P

packed lunch وجبة معلبة *wajba mu'allaba*

page صفحة *safha*

pain ألم *alam*

painkiller مسكن ألم *musakkin alam*

paint صبغ/دهان *sabgh/dihaan*

painting يصبغ *yasbagh*

pajamas بيجامة *biijaama*

palace مكان *makaan*

pan مقلاة *miqlaat*

pane لوح *lawh*

panties سراويل *saraawiil*

pants بنطلون *bantaluun*

pantyhose جورب نسائي *jawrab nisaa'ii*

papaya ببايا *babaaya*

paper ورق *waraq*

paraffin oil زيت البرافين *zayt al-baraafiin*

parasol مظلة *mizalla*

parcel طرد/رزمة *ruzma/tard*

pardon عفوا *'afwan*

parents والدان *waalidaan*

park (gardens) (حديقة) متنزه *mutanazzah (hadiiqa)*

park (verb) يوقف السيارة *yuqif as-sayyaara*

parking garage مرآب سيارات *mir'aab sayyaaraat*

parking space موقف سيارة *mawqif sayyaara*

part (car-) جزء *juz'*

partner شريك *shariik*

party حلفة *hafla*

passable (road) عابر *'aabir*

passenger مسافر *musaafir*

passionfruit غلال الباشين *ghilaal al-bashin*

passport جواز سفر *jawaaz safar*

passport photo صورة جواز *suurat jawaaz*

password كلمة السر *kalimat al-ser*

patient صابر/مريض *mariid/saabir*

pay يدفع *yadfa'*

pay the bill دفع الفاتورة *daf' al-faatuura*

peach دراق/خوخ *khawkh/durraaq*

peanut فستق *fustuq*

pear إجاص *ijjaas*

pearl لؤلؤ *lu'lu'*

peas بازلاء *baazillaa'*

pedal دواسة *dawwaasa*

pedestrian crossing معبر المترجلين *ma'bar al-mutarajjiliin*

pedicure عناية الاقدام *'inaaya al-aqdaam*

pen قلم *qalam*

pencil قلم رصاص *qalam rasaas*

penknife سكين قلم *sikkiin qalam*

penis قضيب *qadiib*

people ناس *naas*

pepper (black) فلفل أسود *fulful aswad*

pepper (chilli) فلفل حار *fulful ḥaar*

performance أداء *adaa'*

perfume عطر *'iṭr*

perhaps ربما *rubbamaa*

period (menstrual) العادة الشهرية *al-'aada ash-shahriyya*

permit رخصة *rukhsa*

person شخص *shakhs*

personal شخصي *shakhsii*

pet حيوان اليف *ḥayawaan aliif*

petrol وقود *waquud*

petrol station محطة وقود *maḥattat waquud*

pharmacy صيدلي *ṣaydaliyya*

phone (هاتف) تلفون *tilifun (haatif)*

phone (verb) يتصل *yataṣil*

phone booth كابينة تلفون *kabiinat tilifun*

phone card بطاقة شحن الرصيد *biṭaqat shahn al-raṣiid*

phone directory دليل هاتف *daliil haatif*

phone number (هاتف) رقم تلفون *raqim tilifun (haatif)*

photo صورة *ṣuura*

photocopier آلة النسخ *aalat an-nasikh*

photocopy نسخة *nuskha*

photocopy (verb) يصور *yuṣawwir*

phrasebook كتاب عبارات *kitaab 'ibaaraat*

pick up (come to) (ياخذ) يتسلم *yatasallam (ya'khudh)*

pick up (go to) (يوصل) يحمل *yaḥmil (yuṣil)*

picnic رحلة *riḥla*

pill (contraceptive) حبوب منع الحمل *ḥubuub man' al-ḥamal*

pills, tablets حبوب *ḥubuub*

pillow مخدة *mikhadda*

pillowcase كيس مخدة *kiis mikhadda*

pin دبوس *dabbuus*

pineapple اناناس *anaanaas*

pipe (plumbing) انبوب *unbuub*

pipe (smoking) غليون *ghalyuun*

pipe tobacco تبغ الغليون *tibgh al-ghalyuun*

pity شفقة *shafaqa*

place of interest اماكن مهمة *amaakin muhimma*

plain (simple) بسيط/صريح *basiiṭ/ sariih*

plain (not flavored) بدون نكهة *biduun nukha*

plan (intention) خطة (برنامج) *khuṭṭa (barnaanaj)*

plan (map) مستوي *mustawii*

plane طائرة *ṭaa'ira*

plant نبات *nabaat*

plaster cast الجبس الطبي *al-jibs at-ṭibbii*

plastic بلاستك *blaastik*

plastic bag كيس *kiis*

plate لوح *lawḥ*

platform منصة *manaṣṣa*

play (drama) مسرحية *masraḥiyya*

play (verb) يلعب *yal'ab*

play golf لعب الغولف *la'ab al-gulf*

playground منطقة لعب للأطفال *minṭaqat la'ib lil-aṭfaal*

playing cards لعب الورق *la'ib al-waraq*

play sports يلعب رياضة *yal'ab riyaaḍa*

play tennis يلعب التنس *yal'ab at-tinis*

pleasant ممتع *mumti'*

please من فضلك *min faḍlik*

pleasure متعة *mut'a*

plug (electric) القابس *al-qaabis*

plum برقوق *barquuq*

pocket جيب *jayb*

pocketknife سكين الجيب *sikkiin al-jayb*

point out يشير الى *yushiir ilaa*

poisonous سام *saam*

police شرطة *shurta*

police officer ضابط شرطة *daabit shurta*

police station مركز الشرطة *markaz as-shurta*

pond بركة *birka*

pony حصان صغير *hisaan saghiir*

population الكثافة السكانية *al-kathaafa as-sukkaaniyya*

pork لحم خنزير *lahm khinziir*

port ميناء *miinaa'*

porter (concierge) بواب *bawwaab*

porter (for bags) حمال *hammaal*

possible ممكن *mumkin*

post (verb) يرسل بالبريد *yursil bil-bariid*

postage اجرة البريد *ujrat al-bariid*

postbox صندوق بريد *sunduuq bariid*

postcard بطاقة بريدية *bitaaqa bariidiyya*

postcode رمز بريدي *ramz bariidii*

post office مكتب بريد *maktab bariid*

postpone يؤجل *yu'ajjil*

potato بطاطس *bataatis*

potato chips مقليات بطاطس *maqliyaat bataatis*

poultry دواجن *dawaajin*

powdered milk حليب مجفف *haliib mujaffaf*

power outlet مخرج الكهرباء *makhraj al-kahrabaa'*

prawn جمبري *jambarii*

precious metal معدن ثمين *ma'dan thamiin*

precious stone حجر ثمين *hajar thamiin*

prefer يفضل *yufaddil*

preference مفضل *mufaddal*

pregnant حامل *haamil*

prescription وصفة *wasfa*

present (gift) هدية *hadiyya*

present (here) موجود *mawjuud*

press (verb) يضغط *yadghat*

pressure ضغط *daght*

price سعر *si'r*

price list قائمة أسعار *qaa'imat as'aar*

print (picture) يطبع *yatba'*

print (verb) يطبع *yatba'*

printer طابعة *tabi'a*

probably محتمل *muhtamal*

problem مشكلة *mushkila*

profession (حرفة) مهنة *mihna (harfa)*

profit (مصلحة) فائدة *faa'ida (maslaha)*

program برنامج *barnaamaj*

pronounce يتلفظ *yatalaffaz*

propane غاز البروبين *ghaaz al-brubiin*

pudding الكعك المحشي *al-ka'ik al-mahshii*

pull يسحب *yashb*

pull a muscle تمطط العضلة *tamattut al-'adala*

pulse نبض *nabd*

pure نقي *naqii*

purify ينقي *yunaqqii*

purple بنفسجي *banafsajii*

purse (for money) جزلان *juzlaan*

purse (handbag) حقيبة *haqiiba*

push يدفع *yadfa'*

puzzle لغز *lughz*

pyramids أهرام *ahraam*

pyjamas بيجامة *biijaama*

Q

quarter ربع *rub'*

quarter of an hour ربع ساعة *rub' saa'a*

queen ملكة *malika*

question سؤال *su'aal*

quick سريع *sarii'*

quiet هاديء *haadi'*

R

radio مذياع (راديو) *midhyaa' (radyu)*

railroad, railway سكة القطار *sikkat al-qitaar*

rain مطر *matar*

rain (verb) تمطر *tumtir*

raincoat معطف مطري *mi'taf matarii*

rape اغتصاب *ightisaab*

rapid سريع *sarii'*

rash متهور *mutahawwir*

rat جرذ *juradh*

raw خام *khaam*

razor blade شفرة حلاقة *shafrat hilaaqa*

read يقرأ *yaqra'*

ready جاهز *jaahiz*

really حقا *haqqan*

reason سبب *sabab*

receipt وصل *wasl*

reception desk الاستعلامات *al-isti'laamaat*

recipe وصفة طهوية *wasfa tahwiyya*

reclining chair كرسي هزاز *kursii hazzaz*

recommend ينصح به *yunsah bihi*

rectangle مستطيل *mustatiil*

red احمر *ahmar*

red wine خمر احمر *khamr ahmar*

reduction إنخفاض *inkhifaad*

refrigerator ثلاجة *thallaaja*

refund إعادة مال *i'aadat maal*

regards تحيات *tahiyyat*

region منطقة *mintaqa*

registered مسجل *musajjal*

relatives أقارب *aqaarib*

reliable موثوق *mawthuuq*

religion دين *diin*

rent out يستأجر *yasta'jir*

repair يصلح *yuslih*

repairs ترميم *tarmiim*

repeat يعيد *yu'iid*

report (police) محضر *mahdar*

reserve يحجز *yahjiz*

responsible مسؤول *mas'uul*

rest استراحة *istiraaha*

restaurant مطعم *mat'am*

restroom مرافق صحية *maraafiq sihhiyya*

result نتيجة *natiija*

retired متقاعد *mutaqaa'id*

return ticket تذكرة ذهاب واياب *tadhkira dhahaab wa iyaab*

reverse (car) يرجع الى الوراء *yurji' ilaa al-waraa'*

rheumatism الم المفاصل *alam al-mafaasil*

ribbon شريط *shariit*

rice (cooked) أرز *aruz*

rice (grain) حبوب الأرز *hubuub al-aruz*

ridiculous سخيف *sakhiif*

riding (horseback) راكب *raakib*

right (correct) صحيح *sahiih*

right (side) يمين *yamiin*

right of way أولوية العبور *awlawiyyat al-'ubuur*

rinse يشطف *yashtif*

ripe ناضج *naadij*

risk خطر *khatar*

river نهر *nahir*

road طريق *tariiq*

roadway طريق *tariiq*

roasted محمص *muhammas*

rock (stone) صقرة *saqra*

roll (bread) رغيف *raghiif*

roof سقف *saqf*

roof rack سقف السيارة *saqf as-sayyaara*

room غرفة *ghurfa*

room number رقم الغرفة *raqim al-ghurfa*

room service خدمة الغرفة *khidmat al-ghurfa*

rope حبل *habl*

route طريق *tariiq*

rowing boat زورق تجديف *zawraq tajdiif*

rubber مطاط *mattat*

rude غير مهذب *ghayr muhadhab*

ruins خراب *kharaab*

run يركض *yarkud*

running shoes حذاء ركض *hidhaa' rakid*

S

sad حزين *haziin*

safe آمن *aamin*

safe (for cash) خزانة حديدية *khizaana hadiidiya*

safety pin دبوس الامان *dabbous al-amaan*

sail (verb) يبيع *yabii'*

sailing boat مركب *markab*

salad سلطة *salata*

sale بيع *bay'*

sales clerk البائع *al-baa'i'*

salt ملح *milh*

same نفس/مشابه *mushaabih/nafs*

sandals (خف) صندل *sandal (khuf)*

sandy beach ساحل رملي *saahil ramlii*

sanitary towel المنديل الصحي *al-mindiil as-sihhii*

satisfied راض *raadin*

Saturday السبت *as-sabt*

sauce مرق *maraq*

saucepan مقلاة *miqlaat*

sauna حمام بخاري *hammaam bukhaarii*

say يقول *yaquul*

scald (injury) حرق *harq*

scales ميزان *miizaan*

scanner ماسح ضوئي *masiih daw'ii*

scarf (headscarf) حجاب *hijaab*

scarf (muffler) قناع *qinaa'*

scenic walk طريق خلاب *tariiq khallaab*

school مدرسة *madrasa*

scissors مقص *miqas*

Scotland اسكتلندا *iskutlandaa*

screw برغي *burghii*

screwdriver مفتاح براغي *miftah baraaghii*

scuba diving الغوص *al-ghaws*

sculpture فن النحت *fann an-naht*

sea بحر *bahr*

search بحث *bahth*

seasick مرض الإبحار *marad al-ibhaar*

seat مقعد *maq'ad*

second (in line) ثاني *thaanii*

second (instant) ثانية *thaaniya*

second-hand مستعمل *musta'mal*

sedative مسكن *musakkin*

see يرى *yaraa*

send يرسل *yursil*

sentence جملة *jumla*

separate منفصل/يفصل *yafsil/munfasil*

September آب *aab*

serious خطير *khatiir*

service خدمة *khidma*

service station محطة بنزين *mahattat banziin*

serviette منديل المائدة *midiil al-maa'ida*

sesame oil زيت السمسم *zayt as-simsim*

sesame seeds سمسم *simsim*

set رزمة/مجموع *majmuua'/ruzma*

sew يخيط *yakhiit*

shade ظل *zil*

shallow ضحل *dahl*

shame عار *'aar*

shampoo شامبو *shambu*

shark قرش *qirsh*

shave يحلق الذقن *yahliq adh-dhaqn*

shaver محلاق كهربائي *mihllaq kahrabaa'ii*

shaving cream معجون حلاقة *ma'juun hilaaqa*

sheet شرشف *sharshaf*

shirt قميص *qamiis*

shoe حذاء *hidhaa'*

shoe polish صبغ حذاء *sibgh hidhaa'*

shop, store متجر/مخزن *makhzan/matjar*

shop (verb) يتسوق *yatasawwaq*

shop assistant بائع *baa'i'*

shopping center مركز تسوق (السوق) *markaz tasawwuq (as-suuq)*

shop window نافذة الدكان *naafidhat ad-dukkan*

short قصير *qasiir*

short circuit دائرة كهربائية *daa'ira karbaa'iyya*

shorts (short trousers) تبان *tubbaan*

shorts (underpants) سروال تحتي قصير *sirwaal tahtii qasiir*

shoulder كتف *katif*

show يري *yurii*

shower دش *dush*

shrimp الروبيان *ruubyaan*

shutter (camera) مصراع *misraa'*

shutter (on window) مصراع *misraa'*

sieve منخل *munkhul*

sightseeing التنزه *at-tanazzuh*

sign (road) علامة *'alaama*

sign (verb) يوقع *yuwaqqi'*

signature توقيع *tawqii'*

silence صمت *samt*

silk سلك *silk*

silver فضة *fidda*

simple بسيط *basiit*

single (only one) واحد *waahid*

single (unmarried) أعزب *a'zab*

single ticket تذكرة واحدة *tadhkirat waahida*

sir سيد *sayyid*

sister أخت *ukht*

sit (be sitting) يجلس *yajlis*

sit down إجلس *ijlis*

size حجم *hajm*

skiing تزلج *tazalluj*

skin جلد *jild*

skirt تنورة *tannuura*

sleep ينام *yanaam*

sleeping car عربة نوم *'arabat nawm*

sleeping pills حبوب منومة _h_ubuub munawwima

sleeve كم kum

slip ينزلق yanzaliq

slippers نعال خفيف nu'aal _kh_afiif

slow بطيء ba_t_ii'

slow train قطار بطيء qi_t_aar ba_t_ii'

small صغير sa_gh_iir

small change عملة صغيرة 'umla sa_gh_iira

smartphone هاتف ذكي hatif _dh_akii

smell رائحة raa'i_h_a

smoke تدخين/دخان du_kh_an/tad_kh_iin

smoked مدخن muda_kh_an

smoke detector منبه دخان munabbih du_kh_aan

snake حية _h_ayya

snorkel أنبوب تنفس مائي unbuub tanaffus maa'ii

snow ثلج _th_alj

snow (verb) تثلج tu_th_lij

soap صابون saabuun

soap powder مسحوق صابون ma_sh_uuq saabuun

soccer كرة القدم kurat al-qadam

soccer match مباراة كرة قدم mubaaraat kurat qadam

social networks شبكات التواصل الاجتماعي _sh_abakaat al-tawa_s_ul al-ijtimaa'ii

socket (electric) مقبس maqbis

socks جوارب jawaarib

soft drink شراب غير كحولي _sh_araab _gh_ayr ku_h_uulii

sole (of shoe) قدم qadam

someone شخص ما _sh_a_kh_s maa

sometimes أحيانا a_h_yaanan

somewhere في مكان ما fii makaanin maa

son إبن ibn

soon حالا _h_aalan

sore (painful) ألم alam

sore (ulcer) إلتهاب ilti_h_aab

sore throat التهاب الحنجرة ilti_h_aab al-_h_injara

sorry آسف aasif

soup شوربة (حساء) _sh_uurba (_h_isaa')

sour حامض _h_aamid

south جنوب januub

souvenir تذكار tid_h_kaar

soy sauce صلصة _s_al_s_a

spanner, wrench مفتاح صواميل miftaa_h_ sawaamiil

spare احتياطي/اضافي i_h_tiyaatii/idaafii

spare parts قطع غيار qita' _gh_iyaar

spare tyre إطار احتياطي i_t_aar i_h_tiyaatii

spare wheel عجلة احتياطي 'ajala i_h_tiyaa_t_iyya

speak يتكلم yatkallam

special خاص _kh_aas

specialist (doctor) اخصائي a_kh_issaa'ii

speciality (cooking) طبخ خاص tab_kh_ _kh_aas

speed limit حد السرعة _h_ad as-sur'a

spell يتلفظ yatalaffa_z_

sphinx أبو الهول abu al-haul

spices توابل tawaabil

spicy حار _h_aar

splinter شظية _sh_aziya

spoon ملعقة mil'aqa

sport رياضة riyaada

sports center مركز رياضي markaz riyaa_d_ii

spot (place) موقع mawqi'

spot (stain) نقطة nuq_t_a

spouse قرين *qariin*

sprain التواء *iltiwaa'*

spring (device) نابض *naabid*

spring (season) ربيع *rabii'*

square (plaza) ساحة *saaha*

square (shape) مربع *murabba'*

square metre متر مربع *mitr murabba'*

squash (game) الإسكواش *al-iskwaash*

squash (vegetable) هريس *hariis*

stadium ملعب *mal'ab*

stain بقعة *buq'a*

stain remover مزيل البقع *muziil al-buqa'*

stairs درج/سلم *sullam/daraj*

stamp طابع *taaba'*

stand (be standing) قف *qif*

stand up قم *qum*

star نجمة *najma*

starfruit الغلال النجمية *al-ghilaal an-najmiyya*

start يبدا *yabda'*

station محطة *mahatta*

statue تمثال *timthaal*

stay (in hotel) يقيم *yuqiim*

stay (remain) يبقى *yabqaa*

steal يسرق *yasriq*

steam بخار *bukhaar*

steel فولاذ *fuulaadh*

stepfather زوج الام *zawj al-um*

stepmother زوجة الاب *zawjat al-ab*

steps خطوات/درجات *darajaat/ khutuwaat*

sterilize يعقم *yu'aqqim*

sticking plaster ضماد لاصق *damaad laasiq*

sticky tape شريط لاصق *shariit laasiq*

stir-fried مقلي *maqlii*

stitches (in wound) غرز *ghuraz*

stomach (abdomen) بطن *batn*

stomach (organ) معدة *ma'ida*

stomach ache ألم المعدة *alam al-ma'ida*

stomach cramps مغص في المعدة *maghas fii al-ma'ida*

stools براز *biraaz*

stop (bus-) (محطة) موقف *mawqif (mahatta)*

stop (cease) يتوقف *yatawaqqaf*

stop (halt) يوقف *yuuqif*

stopover متوقف *mutawaqqif*

store, shop مخزن *makhzan*

storey طابق *taabaq*

storm عاصفة *'aasifa*

straight مستقيم *mustaqiim*

straight ahead مباشرة *mubaasharatan*

straw (drinking) مصاصة شرب *massaasat shurb*

street شارع *shaari'*

street vendor بائع متجول *baa'i' mutajawwil*

strike (work stoppage) إضراب *idraab*

string حبل/خيط *khayt/habl*

strong قوي *qawii*

study يدرس/دراسة *diraasa/yadrus*

stuffed animal حيوان محشو *hayawaan mahshuu*

stuffing الحشو *al-hashuu*

subtitles ترجمة الأفلام *tarjamat al-aflaam*

subway قطار الأنفاق *qitar al-anfaaq*

succeed ينجح *yanjah*

sugar سكر *sukkar*

suit بدلة *badla*

suitcase حقيبة *haqiiba*

summer الصيف *as-sayf*

sun شمس *shamsii*

sunbathe حمام شمسي *hammaam shamsii*

Sunday الاحد *al-ahad*

sunglasses نظارات شمسية *nazzaaraat shamsiyya*

sunhat قبعة شمسية *qubba'a shamsiyya*

sunrise شروق الشمس *shuruuq ash-shams*

sunscreen مرهم ضد الشمس *murham did ash-shams*

sunset غروب *ghuruub*

sunshade وقاء من الشمس *waqaa' min ash-shams*

sunstroke ضربة شمس *darbat shams*

suntan lotion مستحضر إسمرار البشرة *mustahdar ismiraar al-bashara*

suntan oil زيت إسمرار البشرة *zayt ismiraar al-bashara*

supermarket السوق المركزية *as-suuq al-markaziyya*

surcharge أجرة اضافية *ujra idaafiyya*

surf الأمواج المتكسرة *al-amwaaj al-mutakassira*

surface mail البريد العادي *al-bariid al-'aadi*

surfboard لوح التزلج على الامواج *lawh at-tazalluj 'alaa al-muwaaj*

surname اللقب *al-laqab*

surprise مفاجأة *mufaaja'a*

swallow يبلع *yabla'*

swamp مستنقع *mustanqa'*

sweat عرق *'araq*

sweater (بلوز) كلسة *kalsa (bluuz)*

sweet حلو *huluu*

sweetcorn ذرة حلوة *dhura hulwa*

swim يسبح *yasbah*

swimming costume زي سباحة *zay sibaaha*

swimming pool حوض سباحة *hawd sibaaha*

swindle يخدع/خداع *khudaa'/yakhda'*

switch مفتاح *miftaah*

synagogue معبد يهودي *ma'bad yahuudii*

syrup شراب دواء *sharaab dawaa'*

T

table منضدة *mindada*

tablecloth قماش المنضدة *qimaash al-mindada*

tablemat غطاء المنضدة *ghitaa' al-mindada*

tablespoon ملعقة طعام *milaqa'a ta'aam*

table tennis كرة الطاولة *kurat at-taawila*

tablets حبوب *hubuub*

tableware أدوات المائدة *adawaat al-maa'ida*

take (medicine) يأخذ *ya'khudh*

take (photo) يلتقط *yaltaqit*

take (time) يستغرق *yastaghriq*

talk حديث/يتحدث *hadditha/yatahaddath*

tall طويل *tawiil*

tampon سدادة *siddaada*

tanned مدبوغ *madbuugh*

tap حنفية *hanafiyya*

tap water ماء الحنفية *maa' al-hanafiyya*

tape measure شريط قياس *shariit qiyaas*

tassel شرابة *shurraaba*

taste طعم *ta'am*

taste (verb) يذوق yadhuuq

tax ضريبة dariiba

tax-free shop دكان بدون ضريبة dukkaan biduun dariiba

taxi تاكسي (سيارة اجرة) taaksi (sayyaarat ujra)

taxi stand موقف تاكسي mawqif taksii

tea (black) شاي shaay

tea (green) شاي أخضر shaay akhdar

teacup كوب kuub

teapot ابريق شاي ibriiq shaay

teaspoon ملعقة شاي mil'aqat shaay

teat (bottle) حلمة hilma

telephoto lens عدسة جهاز الفوتوغراف 'adasat jihaaz al-futughraf

television تلفزيون tilifizyuun

telex تلكس tiliks

temperature (body) درجة حرارة darajat haraara

temperature (heat) درجة حرارة darajat haraara

temple معبد ma'bad

temporary filling حشوة مؤقتة hashwa mu'aqqata

tender, sore ألم alam

tennis تنس tinnis

ten عشرة 'ashara

tent خيمة kayma

terminus نهاية خط الرحلة nihaayat khat ar-rihla

terrace سطيحة satiiha

terribly بفظاعة bifaza'aa

thank يشكر yashkur

thank you, thanks شكراً shukran

thaw ذوبان dhawabaan

theatre مسرح masrah

theft سرقة sariqa

there هناك hunaaka

thermometer (body) ميزان الحرارة miizaan al-haraara

thermometer (weather) الترمومتر at-tirmumitr

thick سميك samiik

thief لص lis

thigh فخذ fakhidh

thin (not fat) نحيف nahiif

thin (not thick) رقيق raqiiq

think (believe) يظن yazun

think (ponder) يفكر yufakkir

third (1/3) ثلث thuluth

thirsty عطشان 'atshaan

this afternoon بعد ظهر اليوم ba'da zuhr al-yawm

this evening هذا المساء haadhaa al-masaa'

this morning هذا الصباح haadhaa as-sabaah

thread خيط khayt

throat حنجرة hunjura

throat lozenges كراميل الحلق الطبي karaamiil al-halq at-tibbii

thunderstorm عاصفة رعدية 'aasifa ra'diyya

Thursday الخميس al-khamiis

ticket (admission) بطاقة دخول bitaaqat dukhuul

ticket (travel) تذكرة سفر tadhkira safar

ticket office مكتب تذاكر maktab tadhaakir

tidy (ينظم) يرتب yurattib (yunazzim)

tie (necktie) رباط العنق ribaat al-'unuq

tie (verb) (ربط) يشد yashud (yarbit)

tights (thick) سميك samiik

tights (pantyhose) الرداء المحكم ar-ridaa' al-muhakkam

time (occasion) مناسبة *munaasaba*

times (multiplying) (في) ضارب *daarib (fii)*

timetable جدول مواعيد *jadwal mawaa'iid*

tin (can) علبة *'ulba*

tin opener مفتاح علب *miftaah 'ulab*

tip (gratuity) بقشيش/إكرامية *ikraamiyya/baqshiish*

tissues محارم *mahaarim*

tobacco تبغ *tibgh*

today اليوم *al-yawm*

toddler طفل صغير *tifl saghiir*

toe إصبع القدم *isbi' al-qadam*

together مع بعض *maa' ba'd*

toilet التواليت/المرحاض *al-mirhaad/ at-tuwaaliit*

toilet paper ورق التواليت *waraq tuwaaliit*

toilet seat كرسي التواليت *kursii at-tuwaaliit*

toiletries مساحيق *masaahiiq*

tomato طماطم *tamaatim*

tomorrow غدا *ghadan*

tongue لسان *lisaan*

tonight هذه الليلة *haadhihi al-layla*

tool أداة *adaat*

tooth سن *sin*

toothache ألم أسنان *alam asnaan*

toothbrush فرشاة أسنان *furshaat asnaan*

toothpaste معجون أسنان *ma'juun asnaan*

toothpick عود تظيف الاسنان *'uud tanziif al-asnaan*

top قمة *qimma*

torch, flashlight مشعل *mish'al*

total مجموع *majmuu'*

tough خشن *khashin*

tour رحلة سياحية *rihla siyaahiyya*

tour guide دليل سياحة *daliil siyaaha*

tourist class درجة سياحية *daraja siyaahiyy*

tourist information office مكتب معلومات السياح *maktab ma'luumaat as-suyyaah*

tow (يجر) يسحب *yashab (yajur)*

tow cable سلك سحب *silk sahb*

towel منشف *minshaf*

tower برج *burj*

town (مدينة) بلدة *balda (madiina)*

town hall قاعة البلدية *qa'aat al-baladiyya*

toy (دمية) لعبة *lu'ba (dumya)*

traffic حركة المرور *harakat al-muruur*

traffic light إشارة ضوئية *ishaara daw'iyya*

train قطار *qitaar*

train station محطة القطار *mahattat al-qitaar*

train ticket تذكرة سفر بالقطار *tadhkarat safar bil-qitaar*

train timetable مواعيد القطار *mawaa'iid al-qitaar*

translate يترجم *yutarjim*

travel سفر *safar*

travel agent مكتب سفريات *maktab safariyyat*

traveler مسافر *musaafir*

traveler's cheque شيك سياحي *shiik siyaahii*

treatment معاملة *mu'aamala*

triangle مثلث *muthallath*

trim (haircut) تسريحة *tasriiha*

trip رحلة *rihla*

truck شاحنة *shaahina*

trustworthy موثوق *mawthuuq*

try on قس *qis*

tube (of paste) علبة *'ulba*

Tuesday الثلاثاء *ath-thulaathaa'*

tuna التن *at-tinn*

tunnel نفق *nafaq*

turn off (اغلق) أطفيء *atfi' (aghliq)*

turn on (افتح) شغل *shaghil (iftah)*

turn over إقلب *iqlib*

TV تلفزيون *tilifizyuun*

TV guide دليل تلفزيون *daliil tilifizyon*

tweezers ملقط صغير *milqat saghiir*

twin-bedded فراش مزدوج *firaash muzdawaj*

Twitter تويتر *twitter*

typhoon إعصار *i'saar*

tyre إطار *itaar*

tyre pressure مستوى الهواء بالإطار *mustawaa al-hawaa' bil-itaar*

U

ugly قبيح *qabiih*

ulcer قرحة *qurha*

umbrella مظلة *mizalla*

under تحت *tahta*

underpants ملابس داخلية *malaabis daakhiliyya*

underpass عبور سفلي *'ubuur suflii*

understand يفهم *yafham*

underwear ملابس داخلية *malaabis daakhiliyya*

undress يخلع/اخلع *ikhla'/yakhla'*

unemployed عاطل عن العمل *'aatil 'an al-'amal*

uneven متعرج *mut'aarrij*

university جامعة *jaami'a*

unleaded بدون رصاص *biduun rasas*

up (فوق) أعلى *a'laa (fawq)*

upright منتصب *muntasib*

urgent (عاجل) ملح *mulih ('aajil)*

urgently (عاجلا) بالحاح *bi'ilhah ('aajilan)*

urine بول *bawl*

usually عادة *'aadatan*

V

vacate يترك *yatruk*

vacation (إجازة) عطلة *'utla (ijaaza)*

vaccinate يلقح *yulaqqih*

vagina المهبل *al-mahbal*

valid صالح/قانوني *qaanuunii/saalih*

valley وادي *waadii*

valuable ثمين *thamiin*

valuables أشياء ثمينة *ashyaa' thamiina*

van عربة *'araba*

vase مزهرية *mizhriyya*

vegetable خضروات *khudrawaat*

vegetarian نباتي *nabaatii*

vein عرق/وريد *wariid/'irq*

velvet (ناعم) مخمل *makhmal (naa'im)*

vending machine آلة بيع *aalat bay'*

venomous سام *saam*

venereal disease مرض تناسلي *marad tanaasulii*

vertical عمودي *'amuudii*

via عبر *'abra*

video camera كاميرة فيديو *kamiirat viidiu*

video cassette شريط فيديو *shariit viidiu*

video recorder مسجل فيديو *musajjal viidiu*

view منظر *manzar*

village قرية *qarya*

virus فيروس *fairoos*

visa تأشيرة/فيزا ta'shiira (visa)

visit زيارة/يزور yazuur/ziyaara

visiting time وقت الزيارة waqt az-ziyaara

vitamins فيتامينات vitaamiinaat

vitamin tablets حبوب فيتامينات hubuub vitaamiinaat

volcano بركان burkaan

volleyball الكرة الطائرة al-kura at-taa'ira

vomit يتقيأ yataqayya'

W

wait ينتظر/إنتظر intazir/yantazir

waiter نادل مطعم naadil mat'am

waiting room غرفة انتظار ghurfat intizaar

waitress نادلة في مطعم naadila fii mat'am

wake up (افق) ينهض/إنهض inhad/ yanhad (afiq)

Wales ويلز wiiliz

walk (noun) مشي mashii

walk (verb) امش/يمشي yamshii/ imshi

walking stick عكاز 'ukaazi

wall (جدار) حائط haa'it (jidaar)

wallet محفظة نقود mihfazat nuquud

wardrobe خزانة ثياب khizaanat thiyaab

warm دافئ daafi'

warn يحذر yuhadhir

warning تحذير tahdhiir

wash يغسل yaghsil

washing غسيل ghasiil

washing line حبل الغسيل habl al-ghasiil

washing machine (ماكنة غسيل) غسالة ghassala (maakinat ghasiil)

wasp دبور dabbuur

watch ساعة/يشاهد yushaahid/sa'aa

water ماء maa'

waterfall شلال shallaal

waterproof ضد الماء did al-maa'

water-skiing تزلج على الماء tazalluj 'alaa al-maa'

way (direction) طريق tariiq

way (method) طريقة tariiqa

we نحن nahnu

weak ضعيف da'iif

wear يلبس yalbas

weather (الجو) الطقس at-taqs (al-jaw)

weather forecast الحالة الجوية al-haala al-jawwiyya

web browser محرك بحث muharrik bahth

webcam كاميرا kamira

wedding حفل زفاف haflu zafaaf

Wednesday الاربعاء al-arbi'aa'

week أسبوع usbuu'

weekday يوم دوام yawm dawaam

weekend عطلة نهاية الأسبوع 'utlat nihaayat al-usbuu'

weigh يزن yazin

weigh-out يزن yazin

welcome اهلا وسهلا ahlan wa sahlan

well (for water) جيد jayyid

well (good) جيد jayyid

west غرب gharb

wet (مبلل) رطب ratib (muballal)

wetsuit معطف مطري mi'taf matarii

what? ماذا؟ maadhaa?

wheel عجلة 'ajala

wheelchair كرسي مدولب kursii mudawlab

when? متى؟ mataa?

where? أين؟ ayna?

which? أي؟ ayy?

white أبيض abyad

white wine نبيذ أبيض nabiidh abyad

who? من؟ man?

why? لماذا؟ limaadhaa?

wide-angle lens عدسات متسعة الزاوية 'adasaat muttasi'at az-zaawiya

widow أرملة armala

widower ارمل armal

wife زوجة zawja

wind ريح (رياح) riih (riyaah)

window (in room) شباك shubbaak

window (to pay) شباك (مكان الدفع) shubaak (makaan ad-dafi')

windscreen, windshield الزجاجة الامامية للسيارة az-zujaaja al-amaamiyya lis-sayyaara

windscreen wiper ماسحة الزجاجة الأمامية للسيارة maasihat az-zujaaja al-amaamiyya lis-sayyaara

wine نبيذ (كحول) nabiidh (kuhuul)

winter شتاء shitaa'

wire سلك silk

witness شاهد shaahid

woman أمرأة imra'a

wonderful جميل (رائع) jamiil (raa'i')

wood خشب khashab

wool صوف suuf

word كلمة kalima

work عمل (شغل) 'amal (shughl)

working day يوم دوام (يوم عمل) yawm dawaam (yawam 'amal)

worn بالي (ممزق) baali (mumazzaq)

worried قلق qaliq

wound جرح jurh

wrap يلف (يغلف) yaluf (yughallif)

wrench, spanner مفتاح صواميل miftaah sawaamiil

wrist رسغ risgh

write أكتب uktub

write down يكتب (يسجل) yaktub (yusajjil)

writing pad دفتر للكتابة daftar lilkitaaba

writing paper أوراق للكتابة awraaq lilkitaaba

wrong خطأ (غلط) khata' (ghalt)

Y

yarn خيط khayt

year سنة sana

yellow اصفر asfar

yes نعم na'am

yes please نعم من فضلك na'am min fadlik

yesterday يوم أمس yawm ams

you أنت anta (M)/anti (F)

youth hostel مسكن الشباب maskan lish-shabaab

Z

zero صفر sifr

zip رمز ramz

zoo حديقة الحيوانات hadiikatu al-haywaanaat

zucchini كوسة kuusa